LIFT YOUR LIFE

Table of Contents

Introduction 1

The Lift Your Life System 7

Part 1: Lift Yourself

The Happiness Cycle – Take Control Of Your Emotions Today! 38

Massive Motivation – You Can Be Bothered 52

Body Beautiful – Transform Your Body And Health 70

Time Mastery – How To Get 'Enough Hours In A Day' 83

Part 2: Lift Your Life

Relationship Mastery – Start Caring Again 91

The 'Rat Race' – Do What You Love Or Love What You Do. 105

Money Troubles – The Money Secrets You Weren't Told In School 116

Part 3: Lift Your Destiny

Build The New You – It's Time To Live By Design 132

Your Fantastic Future – Your Exciting New Journey 140

The Month That Changed Your Life – Master Life In 30 Days 151

INTRODUCTION

This book contains the tools and strategies you'll need to transform yourself and your destiny. Whilst this may seem an outrageous thing to say, so many people across the world (including myself) have been completely amazed by what can happen when you use proven strategies to take control of your life.

It's time for you to finally take control of your life, starting now. I have the right to say that the information in this book, **when acted upon**, will lift your life because I haven't personally invented anything to create the book. I have merely put together a system that uses a combination of some of the greatest personal development ideas in history.

You may of course think that some of the ideas in this book are 'crazy' or 'would never work'. All I'll say to that is; you have been looking for ways to improve your life and for whatever reason, what you have tried so far hasn't worked so please be open minded and allow the techniques inside this book to change your life for the better.

I want you to imagine an old, slightly shaky rope bridge; you are on one side and the life that you really want is on the other and the only way you can get to the other side is with my help. I want you to picture the fact that it seems a bit crazy to take even the first step but for some reason you really do trust me and you do it. As you take each easy step, it seems less crazy and you become excited by the fact that you are going to get to the other side. When you get there you really do feel grateful and congratulate yourself on taking that crazy first step. **100% of people, who don't take the first step; never get there.**

The book has been designed with the idea in mind that, on average, we only remember 10% of what we have read 2 weeks later. However, that statistic can jump well above 80% when it comes to remembering things that we have written down, visualized and actually DONE. That being said, you will need a pen or a pencil and an active imagination as you go through this book because you are actually going to be **doing things.** (If you have an electronic version of this book use a notepad for the writing exercises) Think of this book as a metaphor for life. What I mean by that is; you cannot build a multi-millionaire dollar company or a stunning physique just by reading about it, you are going to have to **do something.**

The following information is simple by design, it is supposed to be a quick, actionable guide for you to get out of the hole you're in and start your continuous improvement. Certain bits of information will be repeated, *this is deliberate* because there are some things that we need to hear a few times before they stick, aren't there. You'll also notice that the chapters get progressively shorter. I did this because I am just like you; I don't want to be reading long chapter after long chapter. Only 1% of people ever finish the longest self books. *The Lift your Life* will allow you to accelerate as you get towards the end so you can **go out and live the life you design.**

It is crucial to realise that people do not just 'escape their rut' or 'transform their lives' by chance. They achieve predictable results by changing their thought patterns and the things they do, every day. Over the course of this book, I am going to share with you these patterns of thinking and acting and how to use them to improve your life.

> "*It always seems impossible until it is done.*"
> *NELSON MANDELA*

Is it Really Possible for me to Change My Life?

The minute you make the decision to change your life, it is already changed forever. Your life really can change in an instant. That moment you say 'I do', the moment your child was born, the job you nearly didn't apply for. Remember a time now when your life changed in a matter of moments and realise how your ultimate destination in life was completely altered as a result. Imagine the possibilities when you actually take control of these moments and ultimately take control of your life's destination, your destiny.

The strategies contained in *The Lift your Life* are cutting edge. Why? They are a culmination of all of the greatest happiness, success and fulfilment techniques ever created. Every time you take action on the new information you will make small changes. Changes you may not even be aware of. As these changes start to stack up on top of each other you will become aware of how much you have changed and how much your life has improved.

You may not believe every chapter is applicable to you right now. For example, you may be perfectly happy with your career and finances but not so happy with your health and relationships. That's fine, I encourage you to use this book as a guide that you can turn to, to improve any area of your life at any given time. However, I believe that one key to happiness is progress and even if one area of your life is good, it can always improve so why not read the whole book and you may pick up some ideas to make your life even better.

I'm sure you have heard of the benefits of 'persistence'. With a little persistence, you will be just like the rocket that uses eighty per cent of its fuel just to get off the ground. In this universe, big changes need big energy, so be prepared to invest your heart and soul into improving your life and just like the rocket you will climb to heights that were previously viewed as 'impossible'.

When the Wright brothers first suggested the possibility of flight they were seen by their friends and family as "totally insane". Make no mistake, these people were saying this to the inventive brothers out of love and they didn't want them to "waste their time". Luckily for all of us the Wright brothers refused to give in just because 'other people' couldn't see the revolutionary future of air travel that they could. Due to their persistence, a few short years later and after other humans caught on to the 'possibilities' of air travel we can now get from London to New York in 7 hours whilst lying in bed and watching a movie. I cannot help but wonder how many human breakthroughs and opportunities to live extraordinary lives have been quashed my well meaning loved ones.

Countless amounts of people have used the strategies presented in this book to catapult themselves to amazing success and happiness from exactly where you are right now, or even worse situations! There is a catch; however, for the techniques in this book to work I am going to need you to commit to playing at 110%. 80% just won't cut it. You have nothing to lose and everything to gain; be bold, be brave and be fantastic. Finally, be prepared to 'close your ears' to the well meaning advice of other people and stay committed on your journey of self-improvement because some of the ideas may seem crazy at first but hey, so did the aeroplane…

My Story

> *"People will ridicule your journey and then be in awe of your destination"* **JERMAINE HARRIS**

Whilst juggling University, an overactive social life and ever increasing debt, I found myself in the depths of a negative life cycle. I was 'stuck in a rut'. Something was trying to tell me to 'snap out of it' for a good few years: being strapped to a heart monitor from excessive drinking wasn't enough; a near fatal car crash wasn't enough. It wasn't until I nearly lost my leg in a soccer accident that I finally decided 'enough was enough' and I finally acknowledged the fact that my life was in a bad place. I decided: no more negative relationships, no more overspending, no more unhealthy habits, no more dead-end jobs, no more unhappiness. It was time to change.

Harnessing my amazing new energy, Masters Degree level Psychological knowledge and an obsession of studying human potential, I began developing a collection of techniques to turn every area of my life around. I've noticed a huge improvement in every area of my life from my confidence, to my career and even the way people behave towards me. Everything that I've learned and applied in my life and other people's lives, the stuff that really works, is the information you are about to read!

Two whole Years of taking action, a Degree and Masters Degree in Psychology, 300+ books read, hundreds of seminars and webinars attended and more recently; real-life, practical application with my clients has allowed me to be crystal clear on my mission in life.

My purpose in life and the aim of this book is to help you realise how much health, happiness and success you have stored within you and show you how to release it.

I have to say that I am still in the early stages of the journey of self-improvement and I want you to know that only three years ago I had all the same negative feelings and doubts that you have. It is exciting to think you can create your dream life though, isn't it? The best thing that I ever did was to **jump in and go for it,** *you* can do the same.

As you read on I want you to get in touch with the part of yourself that comes alive when you go to see a movie and you let your imagination run wild. I encourage you to do this because at times, some of things that I ask you to do may seem a little 'out-there' but with me as your guide you are going to follow my instructions and reprogram your mind for a whole new positive life!

> *"You don't have to be great to start, but you have to start to be great."* ZIG ZIGLAR

THE LIFT YOUR LIFE SYSTEM

"What the mind of man can conceive and believe, it can achieve" **NAPOLEON HILL**

When I first **decided** to lift my life, I remember just sitting there for a moment and picturing in my mind what it could be like. I saw myself living up to my potential, living in a healthy body, with beautiful relationships and with my dream career.

I'd like you to do the same now. *Stop and vividly imagine in big, bright, HD pictures how your life would look if everything was exactly the way you wanted it to be.*

- What do you see?
- How do you feel?
- What do you hear?
- What does your body look like?
- How amazing is your career?
- What are your relationships like?
- How is your health?
- What are your finances like?

Notice how you feel better already. Your mind doesn't know the difference between a real experience and an imaginary one so the feelings are the same. As you use the strategies in this book you are going to make this vision a reality.

It is important that I make something crystal clear at this point. I am NOT into positive thinking for the sake of positive thinking. To paraphrase Anthony Robbins; I would not walk into your garden and say "there's no weeds' there's no weeds, there's no weeds!" We would get our hands in there and we would rip those weeds out! Exactly the same is true of your life and your mind. With this book as your guide you are going to remove the negativity from your life and your mind and plant 'seeds' of health, wealth and happiness. As these seeds start to grow, you will notice how amazed you are by the positive changes that start to happen in your life.

When I was designing the 'Lift your Life System', I had no idea that it was going to end up looking like a heart and when I realised that this was going to be the case I just stopped and looked at it for a moment. I realised that my mission is help YOU get to a point where you LOVE your life and everything and everyone in it. You will start to love everything about your life as you make progress whilst reading this book, provided that you **DECIDE** that your life is going to change and immediately take **ACTION**.

The Captain and The Crew of Your Marvellous Mind

"Whatever we plant in our subconscious mind and nourish with repetition and emotion will one day become a reality" EARL NIGHTINGALE

To get the most out of the techniques in this book it is vital that you imagine your mind being made up of two areas. One is your conscious mind and the other is your subconscious mind.

Your conscious mind is like the captain of your ship; whilst you are awake it is always analysing, critiquing and thinking 'logically'. If I ask you to **STOP** right now and think of 10 things you know about the USA, you literally have to stop and think about it using your conscious mind.

Your subconscious mind is like the crew of the ship, controlling all of your bodily functions, from your breathing to digesting your food. Your subconscious mind is where everything you have ever seen, heard, tasted, touched or smelled is stored; every memory and every experience. It is in the majesty of your subconscious mind where all of your problem-solving abilities lie as well as every ounce of your intelligence and creativity. If I ask you to **STOP** right now and quickly put your right arm out to the side, you can do it immediately, without having to think of coordinating all of the 130 muscles involved. This is your subconscious mind taking control.

Your subconscious mind allows you to see things differently and solve your problems from a different angle. How many times have you gone to sleep with a problem and woken up with the answer? This is the phenomenon of the 'crew' of your subconscious mind, never sleeping and continuing to work on things whilst you are asleep.

Your subconscious mind is also where your mental habits live. We first learn to do something with our conscious minds and then it gets repeated and repeated until it is totally automatic and the conscious mind becomes less involved and the once new skill can be done 'without thinking'. If you know how to drive a car, you will know exactly how this feels.

However, these skills are not limited to physical acts like driving a car. They can be skills like making ourselves feel bad, indecisiveness, getting stressed out or being paralyzed by fear of failure. They can also be helpful skills of feeling fantastic, motivated, confident and productive. You are going to replace all of the negative ones with positive ones through exciting, emotion filled repetition. Please don't underestimate the power of repetition because your subconscious mind will store that which is repeated by the conscious mind with emotion whether it's good or bad. The only reason you respond to your name is because it was stored in your subconscious mind through repetition. You are going to use this technology by commanding and demanding your subconscious mind to deliver the body, finances, relationships and life that you want.

Decision

> *"It is in your moments of decision that your destiny is shaped"* ANTHONY ROBBINS

I have learned that you will never make positive changes in your life unless you truly DECIDE to make that change no matter what. When you have made a true decision, you have **decided** that it is going to happen for you no matter what. That is why it is at the very top of *The Lift your Life System,* it's the very first step because unless you make that absolute decision you will not make a positive change.

It all started with a decision for all great people; at a very young age Tiger Woods **decided** he was going to be the best golfer in the world, Donald Trump **decided** he was going to have a multi-billion dollar empire, Arnold Schwarzenegger **decided** that he was going to win Mr. Olympia (and indeed achieve many other things after that). I *decided* to write this book and when that that decision was made I had no intention of looking back.

As you read these words, decide that your life is going to be the way you want it to be in a very short space of time. Decide that as you practice the techniques in this book your life is going to improve day by day. Decide to permanently raise your standards in EVERY area of your life because from this point on, anything below that standard is not acceptable! Using your body as an example, what would it be like if you had the standards of a professional athlete? Take a moment to **imagine** that you have these standards when it comes to the way you eat, exercise and take care of your body.

- What does your body look like?

- How do you feel?

- What are people saying to you about your body?

It is easy to see that **deciding** to permanently raise your standards can have a very profound effect on your life in a very short space of time.

Stop and Write it Down

There are going to be various times in this book when I ask you to stop and write something down. This serves two purposes. Firstly it will make the reading experience easier and you will stay focused. Secondly, writing things down 'imprints' the ideas into your subconscious mind.

Write down an area of your life in which you are going to permanently raise your standards. Write down how it will feel to be living with this new high standard.

_____
_____
_____
_____
_____
_____
_____
_____

Role Models

"A role model is a mentor, someone you can learn from on a daily basis" **DENZEL WASHINGTON**

Finding people that have already achieved the result that you want to achieve can cut the time it takes to achieve your goals or your dream life in half! Why would you want to learn from years and years of mistakes when you can learn from other people's mistakes? When I first discovered this idea I really started to love it. There are books written, videos recorded and classes taught that are very affordable and readily available from people that have already done what you are trying to do! Why not just do what they did; it seemed to work didn't it? How many musical performers have dance moves that look a lot like Michael Jackson's? The answer is a lot because he revolutionized performing and got such phenomenal feedback for his dancing it was inevitable that other people would adopt some of his style.

Adopt the **mindset** and take the **action** of the people you'd love to be like and great things are about to happen in your life. Learn about how they think; if they have book, read it. Find out how they got that body or made that business work or achieved their goals and you can do the same. It would be great to get the same results in life as your heroes, wouldn't it?

Role models can also help you to realise that it's possible. If they can do it, you can do it! You will see the story of Roger Bannister being a metaphor for this idea everywhere but it is such a startling illustration of the phenomenon that it has to be mentioned here as well. Scientists and other experts used to say that running the 4 minute mile was not only "dangerous" but "impossible". In the 1940's the record for running the mile stood at 4.01 and people started to believe that the human body had reached its limit. In 1954 Roger Bannister broke the 4 minute barrier. Within six weeks someone else had done it, now over one thousand people have done it including high school kids! What changed? First and foremost Roger Bannister had to **believe** it was possible; he was repeating the **images in his mind** of him actually achieving the feat. Once this vision became a reality for Roger Bannister it was automatically proved to everybody else that it was *possible*. The belief about running the 4 minute mile had changed and there was a **role model** that had shown the way.

I'd be honoured if you would let be your mentor when it comes to lifting your life. I can help you have a great life now and in the future. All I ask is that you continue to **believe** and keep a laser **focus** on improving your life because as you'll realise as you read these pages, what you focus on expands.

Stop and Write it Down

Pick someone who has characteristics that you admire and would love to emulate. What is it about them makes you admire them? What are the best ways for you to learn how to do what they do so well?

_____
_____
_____
_____
_____
_____
_____

Now I want you to picture this person in your mind, doing the things that you admire them for. How do they move? How do they breathe? How do they think? What do they see? What do they hear?

Now imagine stepping into their body and notice how great it feels to merge all of your amazing characteristics with theirs. Feel yourself doing the things that they do and notice how you grow in confidence as you realise you can be just as great as they are.

[TAKE A BREAK]

Every 10 pages or so you'll see the words 'take a break' just like the ones above. I have done a lot of reading over the past 5 years and I know how difficult it can be to hold your concentration for long periods of time. So when you see 'take a break'- jump up, have a stretch, have a glass of water, watch your favourite funny video, listen to your favourite song; do whatever you have to do to relax, refocus and be ready to get going again.

Beliefs

"If you don't change your beliefs, your life will be like this forever. Is that good news?" W. MAUGHAM

It is your beliefs that can hold you down, keep you where you are and stop you from even attempting to improve your life. How often do you hear people say things like "I've tried *everything* to lose weight" or "No matter what I try, I just can't get out of debt"? Do you think that those people have tried "EVERYTHING" to lose weight or get out of debt? Of course they haven't, the chances are they have tried the same 3 or 4 things that don't work. As a result they have started to **believe** that this is true for them. If you hold onto this type of belief your mind will do whatever it takes to prove itself right and you'll stay stuck for the rest of your life.

However, beliefs do also have the ability to build us up and take us to heights that we can only imagine. Imagine you **decided** to **believe** that from this moment on you were destined to live beyond 100 years of age and be in amazing, vibrant shape deep into your old age? How would your day-to-day living change? Would you eat well? Would you exercise? Would you be relaxed more often? Again, your mind would do everything to prove itself right in line with this belief.

The challenge is that beliefs are merely how you interpret an event and if these events are MIS-interpreted then we could potentially have a disempowering belief that negatively impacts our life. For example, take two people that are bullied from a young age in school; how is that one becomes a bully and one becomes a charitable, people person? The answer is clear, it is not 'what happens to us'; it is our 'interpretation and response to what happens' that makes the difference.

When I **decided** that I was going to run a half-marathon for Cancer Research I had to tear down some disempowering beliefs. I had been told all my life that my asthma was negatively impacting my cardiovascular fitness and more recently that the titanium rod and screws in my leg would mean I couldn't run more than a mile on a hard surface. I had fallen victim to other people's opinions as opposed to *creating my own life*. I had made other people's opinions my beliefs and this is very easily done if you do not stand guard at the door of your mind. Take note of the words of motivational speaker Les Brown: "Someone's opinion of you does not have to become your reality!"

How do you break down a disempowering belief and replace it with and empowering one? **Change the picture you're holding in your mind.** I realised that when I believed that I couldn't run long distances I was holding pictures in my mind of me doubled over in pain with my leg and struggling to breathe. I began training my mind to **see** myself crossing the finishing line feeling healthy, happy, proud and in control. I did this EVERY DAY until my mind accepted it as reality and I now **believed** that it could be done.

Everything that was ever created, everything that you see around you right now; including this book, began as a picture in someone's mind.

Stop and Write it Down

Write down *everything* that you believe about life, other people, your happiness, motivation, health, body, money, relationships, career and your future

_____
_____
_____
_____
_____
_____
_____
_____
_____
_____
_____

Now go back and divide the beliefs into 'beliefs that help me' and 'beliefs that hurt me'. With the beliefs that 'help you' I want you to make them even stronger and write them down in their new improved way. For example: "I believe that people like me because I am friendly" could become "I am totally certain that people love me because I am loving, caring and generous in every relationship I create".

_____
_____
_____
_____
_____
_____
_____
_____
_____
_____
_____
_____
_____
_____
_____
_____
_____
_____
_____
_____
_____

Decide that you are no longer willing to hold on to the 'beliefs that hurt you' and you are only ever going to repeat and hold in your mind 'beliefs that help you'. With practice this about to change your life.

You are about to realise that no one can tell you what something means and you can choose to believe whatever you want, can't you. Over time, you will notice that you are just focused on solutions to problems rather than the problems themselves.

Living from this place of strength means that you are big enough to deal with whatever comes your way. You will start to take **action** on the things you want from life because you now **believe it's possible.** This means that you have lifted your life already because you now **believe** that everything is happening in your favour and it is all part of the process. **Believe** that small improvements every single day are inevitable and this will ultimately make your life the way you want it to be.

Habits

> *"Successful people are simply those with successful habits"* BRIAN TRACY

The results that we get in our lives are largely dictated by our habits. Think about it: if you don't eat or drink too many sugary substances and clean and floss your teeth every day, the result is that you have got healthy, bright, white teeth. If you don't clean and floss your teeth every day the result is that your teeth have cavities and are rotting.

It is absolutely essential that if we want the successful result that we have the successful habits to create it. How often do you hear people say things like "I need to lose weight" and then you see those people eating fatty unhealthy foods every day? The result you want; a healthy great looking body is impossible when the eating habits are unhealthy.

What can you get in the habit of doing that will accelerate your progress? This is where it all started for me and I soon realised that one good habit is like a magnet for another and soon you'll be doing healthy, happy, empowering things every day.

A way to fast track this is to find a **role model** and ask them what their habits are and how they've achieved the result that you want and then you can replicate those habits. Within the following chapters I'll reveal the habits that have worked for me in each area of my life and ultimately, how easy it is to make the change.

Stop and Write it Down

Realise, you are not a robot. You are a magnificent human being and you can take control of your daily actions. Have some fun now and laugh as you write down and realise some things that you do on a regular basis that you know are not good for you but you still do them without thinking?

_____
_____
_____
_____
_____
_____
_____

Decide, that from now on you are going to consciously, take control of the things that you do a daily basis until the things that you do on 'autopilot' contribute directly to you having a better life. The bonus to this lifestyle is that 'treats' mean so much more. Let's say you were improving your health and you decided stop eating chocolate every day without thinking. How much more fulfilling would it be those one or two times a month when you treated yourself to a bar of chocolate knowing you are living in a healthy, great looking body?

Discipline

> *"To enjoy good health, to bring true happiness to one's family, to bring peace to all, one must first discipline and control one's own mind"* **BUDDHA**

The concept of discipline is very easy to grasp and everything that you are about to read you probably already 'know' but you don't truly *know it* unless you *LIVE IT!*

To live with true discipline you have to have taken the very first step and **decided** to get a particular result. If you have made a true **decision** then the discipline will automatically follow. Just a like that rocket that uses eighty per cent of its fuel to leave planet earth you will require the highest levels of discipline for the first ten to twenty days after you have decided to make change. Have the discipline to follow this book through to the end and positively change your life and you will have started to build the **habit** of being disciplined. Discipline builds more discipline. Simple concept isn't it.

Knowledge

"Knowledge is only potential power until it comes into the hands of someone who knows how to get himself to take effective action." ANTHONY ROBBINS

I believe that we should always be on a continuous quest for knowledge. However, why is it that there are so many people that have so much knowledge yet they do not have the life that you would expect them to have? I'll give you a personal example; I was fully educated on the fact that eating and drinking a lot of dairy was having a negative effect on my asthma for many years, so why did I keep doing it? Knowledge is absolutely worthless unless acted upon! 65% of people reading this book will read some or most of it and then do absolutely nothing. 30% of people will read it and then make positive changes for a week or two and then go backwards. 5% of people will read the information in this book and then take **persistent**, continuous **action** on it for the rest of their lives and ultimately end up living the life they desire. I don't give you those statistics to be negative, it's just real and the funny thing is I have been part of all three groups but I've now realised that life can be a lot more fun and you can make faster progress if you are part of the 5%. Decide to be part of the 5% right now and make rapid progress.

The knowledge about what you want to achieve will ALWAYS be available. However, the **decision** to **act** on the knowledge can only come from you.

Goals

> *"Set your goals high and don't stop till you get there"*
> BO JACKSON

Goal setting can get you what you want! Simple as that, and if goals don't get you *exactly* what you what you from life, the pursuit of worthy goals will transform you into a person that you had no idea you were capable of becoming anyway! Goals really have changed my life and I have achieved things I had no idea I was capable of and I have certainly become a person that I had no idea that I could be. I was shocked to learn that only 20% of people actually set goals and only 6% of people ever achieve their goals, or make progress as a person.

I have personally used an almost 'obsessive' study of human potential, success and personal development literature to devise what I believe to be the most effective way to set goals. I call it 'The 4Wheel Drive Method^{TM}'. There are 4 'W's' in the 4 wheel drive method that represent the wheels on a 4x4 vehicle and just like a 4x4 vehicle when you have all of these wheels working together to help you set and achieve goals, no terrain is too difficult. At the moment you may have goals that are okay if all is going well, but what if you have to 'go off road' and tackle some tough situations? The 4Wheel Drive Method^{TM} will take care of that for you.

The 4 W's

The 4 "W's":

'What do I want, EXACTLY?'

'Why EXACTLY do I want it?'

'When EXACTLY do I want it by?'

'What MUST I do to get it?'

Let's start with **'What do I want, EXACTLY?'** – If you don't define what it is that you want, exactly; then your mind has no idea how to get you there. If you wanted to drive to your hotel in Paris from London, would you find the exact address of the hotel or would you just type 'FRANCE' into the satellite navigation system? Your brain works the same way; it needs to know EXACTLY where you want to go. A lot of the time people are setting loose goals and achieving them. How often have you heard someone say "I want to lose some weight" and when they only lose a pound they are disappointed. How can they be disappointed when they have achieved their goal!?

The MOST IMPORTANT wheel is: **'Why EXACTLY do I want it?'** You need to know WHY you want to achieve whatever it is that you want to achieve and it has to be powerful enough to get you to do the things that you have to do EVEN when you don't feel like doing them. For example, let's say that you wanted to lose 5lbs of body fat: if the 'Why' was *"So I can fit into my birthday dress"* this may create some leverage but it is only likely to be short term and you will probably put the 5lbs back on after your birthday. What if the 'Why' was: *"So I can be the best version of myself* *humanly possible, remaining healthy vibrant and energetic every single day, enabling me to do more, be more and have more. Giving me more years with my children, grand-children and great grand children and inspiring them along the way"* – Do you see how this 'Why' is far more likely to create leverage and create lasting change?

Next is **'When EXACTLY do I want it by?'** Your brain needs an exact date to get you to take enough action at the right times. To use the holiday analogy again, imagine you said: "we're going on holiday next summer" and left it at that. How would you know when to go shopping for the items you needed? How would you know when to pack? The answer is; you wouldn't! That is why the reality is you'd be saying something like: "we're going to Madrid on the 17th July 2014". You're brain would know that it has to do everything that it needs to do in preparation for the trip. Goals are the same.

The final element is: **'What MUST I do to get it?'** This wheel has the most freedom out of all of the wheels because you may not know everything that you have to do to achieve the goals but it will be vital for you to take an abundance of action and start as soon as possible! It is important that you work out what you are going to do first and find a plan, a mentor or a strategy but the most important thing is to GET MOVING!

Be careful when planning what to do to get it because if you know EVERYTHING that you have to do to achieve the goal, you won't take enough action because you won't be inspired. It'll be 'too easy'.

Putting it all together

Once you have gone through the above process of creating a goal you are left with something that should be phrased like the example below. Note, that the goal is stated in the PRESENT TENSE and in such a way that provokes positive feelings of it already being achieved; this magnetizes the subconscious mind to everything you'll need to do to achieve the goal. Once you have all of your goals written out this way it is important to review them at least once a day and I will go into detail on how to do this a little later.

Here is a goal that I recently achieved that will show you how it can be phrased:

"It is October 6th 2013 and I am so happy grateful that I easily completed the Cardiff half marathon in less than 2 and a half hours in honour of my dear Grandfather and in support of Cancer Research UK. This is an amazing achievement for me and it serves as a signpost in my life that I am over the leg break that I suffered and I no longer suffer from asthma. I feel healthy, vibrant and energized by the achievement and it has given me an insight into how I can achieve whatever I put my mind to."

[TAKE A BREAK]

Physiology, Focus & Mind Images

"The only limits in life are the ones we impose on ourselves" BOB PROCTOR

It is quite possible that if you are feeling down and de-motivated about life on a regular basis that you *making yourself* feel that way.

Think for a moment of the golfer who straight after he hits the poor shot immediately and almost proudly states "I knew that I was going to put that in the water!" How did they know? Because as they gingerly approached the ball, they felt unhappy about hitting the shot and they 'watched' it in go in the water in their minds before they even swung the club.

The chain of negative processes can then continue when we start speaking to ourselves in a way that we would never speak to anybody, ever! We say things like: "You are such an idiot! Why can't you do anything right?" It is easy to see how negative states are pretty much guaranteed if we approach life and situations like this on a regular basis.

So what are you supposed to do about this? How can you choose to be happy and control your state? It is very simple, take conscious control over the most powerful computer in the universe, your mind and make it a **habit** to take control of the way you move, the images you make in your minds and the way you talk to yourself.

You could start by making a conscious, deliberate determined effort to hold yourself as if you were the happiest person in the world and your biochemistry will follow suit. How do would you be holding your body if you were 100% confident in yourself, with the body of your dreams and financially free? Where would your shoulders be? Where would your head be? How would you be breathing?

You can start moving like this *right now*. Start conducting yourself as if all of your goals have already been achieved. Somebody who is a happy success, like Richard Branson, for example, moves his body in a very different way to someone who is depressed. **Decide** that you are no longer willing to hold yourself in that timid, depressed position, ever. The minute you start to feel your shoulders or head start to drop, take **action** immediately and readjust your body. Move, dance, jump up and down; do whatever it takes to change your physiology no matter how silly it feels because if you don't you could be on a downward spiral of feeling extremely negative.

When you're walking around with your shoulders back, chest up and head up your mind 'feels' like you are in control and it **believes** that you are the type of person that can go out and achieve your goals.

'E-MOTION' is created by motion, it is vital that you take this on board. Think about it for a moment, have you ever been jumping up and down with a huge smile on your face and felt the feeling of sadness at the same time? What about when your favourite sports team has scored a goal or a point, how do you move your body?

If you are making yourself feel down you are probably not just holding yourself in a negative way but you are also holding negative pictures in your mind and focusing on the wrong things by asking yourself disempowering questions.

I'd like you to think of the worst movie you have EVER watched. Would you watch it again? Of course not; so why is it that when something bad happens to us we relive it and watch it and relive it watch it over and over again? Just wipe the screen of your mind and CHOOSE to hold an image in mind that makes you feel good.

Finally, be extra vigilant about what you are saying to yourself. Successful entrepreneur John Assaraf said "be very careful what you say to yourself, someone important is listening….YOU!" How many of us know someone who says things like "These things ALWAYS happen to me" or "I'm so unlucky". We have to be very careful about what we say becoming self fulfilling prophecies, unless of course you say "I'm ALWAYS happy, healthy and confident!"

I am very passionate about you taking the **action** to take control of your state, because it is something that will improve the quality of your life *straight away*. With practice, if you notice yourself slipping into a negative physiology with negative mind images and poor self-talk and you'll be able to take control straight away!

Action, Persistence & New Strategy

> *"Our greatest weakness lies in giving up. The most certain way to succeed is to try one more time"*
> **THOMAS EDISON**

When you have your new belief that you can achieve anything that you want to achieve it is imperative that you take constant action towards making your dreams become a reality. A lot of people will talk about visualizing your goals and holding pictures in your mind and that is crucial but what if you visualized yourself as owning a Fortune-500 company but then you sat around on the couch all day, watching TV? It just wouldn't happen. Whatever you **decide** to achieve throughout the course of this book, make sure that you take the **action** required to make it happen, otherwise all of the mindset improvement will just be a waste of time.

Be aware of the fact that it is rare for huge success to fall in your lap; a certain amount of **persistence** is inevitable. Keep going, keep going and keep going until you get there. As I sit and write this book I have not achieved my dream life yet, it has drastically improved but there are still many dreams to make a reality. The great thing about being persistent is you know that you're going to achieve your goals because you're not going to stop UNTIL you do!

It is important to note here that you have to be careful not to persist in doing the things that have been proven not work. Find as many new strategies as you need to until your goal is achieved.

A CONTRACT WITH YOURSELF

It is time to imprint your intent onto your subconscious mind by signing your name to a declaration that states you are committed to improving your life:

I _____,

Hereby commit to the decision I have made to improve my life. I will only entertain beliefs that help me. My habits will be habits that contribute directly to my health, wealth and happiness. I will have fun being disciplined in every area of my life. I will be on a constant quest for knowledge. I will set and achieve goals that get me excited every day. I will use my body, mind and inner voice to create amazing feelings and emotions every day. I will take action, every day towards achieving my goals and I will be persistent on my journey to find the strategies that will make my dreams become a reality.

Signed,

_____

Congratulations and thank you for coming this far, you have just finished the longest chapter in the book and you now understand the tools you need to turn your life around. As you improve every area of your life you will notice how each part of the Lift your Life system is involved at different times and these will often be highlighted in **bold** so you can really be aware of the system working for you. Let's have some fun and make your dreams a reality...........

Part 1

LIFT YOURSELF

THE HAPPINESS CYCLE – TAKE CONTROL OF YOUR EMOTIONS TODAY!

"Most folks are as happy as they make up their minds to be."
ABRAHAM LINCOLN

Insert image Item number:

184703448

The Cars, the clothes, the Holiday Homes,
This man had it all.
He spent his life in Party Mode,
It just seemed like a ball!

He had a massive business,
A trophy wife as well,
Famous for his intellect
But for him; ever day was hell.

It all became too much,
He had nowhere else to turn
There was one crucial secret,
That he didn't get to learn.

His success was plain for all to see,
The champagne was always swishing,
But instead of what he had
He focused on what was missing…

What is the key to happiness?

It's not money otherwise all millionaires would be happy. It's not having a great body; otherwise all professional athletes would be happy. It's not being in a relationship otherwise all married people would be happy. It's not having a 'good job' otherwise all doctors and lawyers would be happy. So what the heck is it? I believe that two of the primary keys to happiness are *being happy now* by focusing on what you have and making constant progress.

It has become so obvious to me over the years that it is not what happens to us that determines whether we are happy or not. It is how we respond to what happens. That is why the very first part of this book addresses happiness, because without **deciding** to be happy first, success in any other area of life becomes 'empty success'.

It's Not The Way It's *'Supposed'* To Be

How is it that two women can weigh 250 pounds and one is depressed and feels 'ugly' and the other feels like she is 'sexy and *working it*? It is because the one who feels depressed has a picture in her mind of what she '*should* look like' and it is not the way she is right now. This inevitably means that she will feel unhappy. The woman who feels sexy also has a picture in her mind of what 'sexy' *should* look like and she looks exactly like that so she is happy.

This is true across all areas of life; if you took one of world's wealthiest billionaires and made them, merely a millionaire over night they would be totally devastated. However, if I made you a millionaire over night you'd probably very 'happy', wouldn't you.

The Danger of The Word 'When'

"Happiness doesn't depend on any external conditions; it is governed by our mental attitude."
DALE CARNEGIE

One of the first things that I discovered and now teach is never to use the phrase "I'll be happy when..." You have either said, or heard people say at least one of these things: "I'll be happy when I get more money", "I'll be happy when I lose some weight", "I'll be happy when meet someone". Whenever you are saying "I'll be happy when..." you are training yourself to base your happiness on things that are coming rather than things that you have in the present moment. What this means is you will never be happy. As bleak as that may sound, you can make an immediate change just by changing ONE WORD in the sentence...

Stop and Write it Down

Complete the sentences below with as many things as you can. Let everything flow out of you from the roof over your head to your ability to see; include everything:

I am Happy because

_____

I am Happy because

_____

I am Happy because

_____

I am Happy because
_____

I am Happy because
_____

I am Happy because
_____

I am Happy because
_____

I am Happy because
_____

I am Happy because
_____

I am Happy because
_____

You have just written down 10 reasons as to why you are happy right now. You will have reasons to be happy every day; you just don't **focus on them**. By focusing on the sentence "I am happy because…" every day you will train your brain to look for reasons to *be happy right now*. Once you start being happy right now you are no longer chasing happiness because you think you want certain things in your life. When you are happy now, you will go after the things that you actually want and you will be better at going after them because whatever you are doing whilst you are unhappy, you can bet your last penny on the fact you're going to do a better job now you're happy!

Move To the Positive Side of The Street

"Once you replace negative thoughts with positive ones, you'll start having positive results." WILLIE NELSON

I can promise you right now that your life will never be the same again when you realise that NO ONE CAN CONTROL WHAT YOU THINK. It may take a little **discipline and persistence** at first but when you take responsibility for your happiness and control the **images** and sounds that are going on in your mind happiness is inevitable.

When I say you to you think of a feather right now you don't think the letters 'F-E-A-T-H-E-R' you have a **picture** of a feather on the screen of your mind. Realising that you have control of this is incredible, try this now and let the images come in to your mind: think of a black cat, now think of a polar bear, now think of a sandy desert…Amazing isn't it? The image on the screen of your mind actually changes. **Now think about someone you love with all your heart, make the picture big, bright and detailed. Allow a smile to dance into your eyes and then smile a big smile as you think about them.**

The thought of this person makes you feel happy doesn't it? Wouldn't it be marvellous if you had five or six thoughts like this that you could picture in your mind that would make you feel happy at any given moment? The good news is you can!

Stop and Write it Down
Describe in detail the picture you see in your mind of five people or things in your life that make you happy just by thinking about them.

The real magic occurs when you develop the **discipline** to be able to realise that you are having a 'down moment' and then picture the things that you have just written down to bring yourself back into a happy state. As you do this more and more, you will find yourself flicking through your 'happiness catalogue' automatically. Persist with this and I promise you that it will change your life because you will have taken control of your moment to moment happiness which I believe is the greatest success of all.

See It as It Is But Not Worse!

Each and every one of us has been hit by 'life'. Of course we have. We've been left by people we love when we've done everything right, bills we haven't been able to pay on time, jobs that we have lost, loved ones that have suddenly passed away. It really does feel like we can't make it through the day sometimes, but we usually do.

We (myself included) have fallen into the trap of making the situation seem totally dire with an inevitable, catastrophic ending. However, 99% of these 'catastrophes' never arise. I know people that have been struggling to pay a mortgage payment and all of a sudden they are jumping all the way into predicting the loss of the house. The fascinating thing is these people are still living in the same houses years later. What's happening here? They are getting themselves consistently worked up about a challenge they have been able to overcome again and again and yet they still continue to talk about the 'worst case scenario'.

It is essential that you develop the skill of immediately focusing on solutions to your current challenge and not waste precious 'mental energy' imagining all of the other bigger challenges that could result from the situation that you are facing right now.

Stop and Write it Down

Think about a challenge you are facing in your life right now and answer the following, solution focused questions(it may be difficult at first, but keeping ask yourself the questions and your mind will be compelled to give you an answer):

What is the best thing about this situation?
_____
_____
_____
_____

What is not perfect yet?
_____
_____
_____
_____

What am I willing to do to improve the situation?
_____
_____
_____
_____

What am I no longer willing to do that is keeping me in this situation?
_____
_____
_____
_____

What is the best way for me to have fun along the way as I do everything required for me to improve the situation?

_____

_____

_____

_____

[TAKE A BREAK]

Help Someone Else

> *"There is no exercise better for the heart than reaching down and lifting people up."* JOHN HOLMES

Whatever situation you are in, there is someone not too far away from you that is worse off than you are. Find someone or a group of people that are in a worse situation than you are and help them in whatever way that you can. Kindness is not a one way street. Have you noticed that every time you do something that makes someone feel good, you feel good as well?

Helping someone else is such a wonderful way to improve someone else's life and help you in the process. This can almost become like a 'positive addiction' because any pain you are experiencing begins to fade away as you ease someone else's. You will feel 'happy' in the knowledge that you have made a difference in someone else's life and your focus will be away from your own struggles.

Turn That Frown Upside Down

I know that it sounds like a cliché but just smiling can have a seriously dramatic effect on making you feel happier. You can couple this with changing **the way you hold your body** and the way you use your voice. Have you ever experienced a person with their head held high, their chest up and their shoulders back with a huge smile on their face frantically telling you how 'down in the dumps' they are? I didn't think so. When people are telling you how sad they are; their shoulders are hunched, their head is down, their facial expression is glum and they are speaking slowly because they know that *saying* what is wrong is even more difficult.

The body and mind are constantly linked and one is always affecting the other. What if we could use this to our advantage? People only think that great things happening in the mind affect the body but that's not true. You can make amazing improvements in the way that you feel by radically changing your body. The best thing about this is you can catch it early. The minute that you find yourself sitting or standing in negative way, you can immediately take **action**.

You can put a big smile on your face, throw your shoulders back and look up and your mind is not wired to allow you feel depressed in this state. You'll notice how much better you feel. This is another process where you have to re-train your mind and body and believe me, the **persistence and discipline** will pay off because you will be in charge of the way that you feel.

Words Are Powerful

What you say out loud and in your head will expand in your life. The more you talk about a thing the more you are attracting it into your life. Think about this for a moment: do the people who always talk about debt ever get out? Do the people who always talk about being overweight ever get the body they want? Do the people who moan about their children's behaviour ever control it? Do the people who always say they are unhappy ever get happy?

Now that you have **decided to be happy** and you are serious about it, you are going to have to start taking control of the things you say. You have to decide to speak well of yourself and stop unnecessarily putting yourself down. You are not pretending you are perfect here, you are simply realising that it cannot possibly be helpful to allow the sound of you moaning about your job, family, friends and everything else to vibrate through your body.

When we think about what we have learned about the subconscious mind this makes taking control of the words that we are using even more important. The words that we are saying with emotion are always finding their way into our subconscious minds and staying there and ultimately becoming part of our character.

You are probably 'trying' to improve your life, right? You're 'trying' to lose weight, you're 'trying' to improve your finances and you're 'trying' to be happy. Imagine for a moment what life would be like if you stopped 'trying' to do things and you just did them. If you are **persistent and disciplined** with yourself to eliminate the word 'try' from your vocabulary then you will train your mind to be someone who **decides** to do something and then **does them**.

Progress, Progress, Progress

To be happy as often as possible I truly **believe** that it is important to commit to making constant progress. No matter what endeavour you are involved with from sport to business, you have to keep improving to 'keep up'. Making constant progress is an amazing vehicle for happiness. I often hear people say things like "why does Oprah keep working, surely she has enough money?" Oprah is clearly committed to constantly making progress; she touches more and more people every year and is always expanding on her ideas to serve people in more abundant and diverse ways.

I have worked with professional athletes to make sure that they set goals after their retirement; otherwise they are setting themselves up for feeling unhappy. They have to have something to **focus** on that they can make progress towards. The same is true for you and this is another reason why **goals** are so important.

Win The Day

You don't have to achieve some huge '90 day goal' to be making progress. Commit to making the most of a given 24 hour period. Do a little more than you did yesterday. If you went for a 15 minute walk around the block yesterday and you go for a 16 minute walk today; you have made progress. Keep score of everything that you do so you can track your progress then you will always be able to see how far you have come as opposed to how far you have to go.

FUTURE TRUTH

Have you ever told someone with absolute authority that you were going to achieve some goal or dream, only for them to kill your enthusiasm by saying something like "don't lie to yourself" What if you were just **telling the truth in advance?**

Every so often, I am going to ask you stand up put your hand your heart and *tell the truth in advance.* I call these 'Future Truths'. You are going to say each future truth with such passion and enthusiasm (not necessarily loud) that it vibrates through your whole body. You are going to hold your body in a way that you would be holding it if it was absolute reality. That being said here is your first one:

WARNING: If you don't want to improve your life then you don't have to do this. It may feel weird but do it on your own and you don't have to worry about what anybody thinks because they never need to know.

> ***"I am so happy and grateful for everything that I have right now. I choose to be happy because I am always in control of what I focus on."***

MASSIVE MOTIVATION – YOU CAN BE BOTHERED

"Be miserable. Or motivate yourself. Whatever has to be done, it's always your choice." DR. WAYNE DYER

INSERT IMAGE Item number: 155425535

How do you get motivated?
The young apprentice asked.
"Ah this is a crucial lesson,
For your Goals to be surpassed!"

I'll ask you a question,
As you've started aiming higher
What would you do if you woke up one night,
And your house was on fire?

Would you take some to psyche yourself up
And wait for motivation to grow?
Or would you jump up out of bed,
Grab your family, take a deep breath and go?

People wait for January,
Like motivation is a 'Season'
But really and truly; like the fire
All you need is a big enough reason...

A few weeks after I had made my **decision** to turn my life around, I had hundreds of sheets of paper with notes about 'how to improve your life' on them. I really wanted to get myself going and when I started to analyze the notes that I had on motivation it seemed that setting **goals** was something that kept coming up.

I was constantly reading about how the most motivated people in the world were people who set goals, and impressive goals at that. Think about it, does the British runner, Mo Farah run over one hundred miles per week because he is just going through the motions or does he do it because he has the goal of winning Olympic medals?

Setting goals is the one thing that got me going and setting and pursuing goals still gets me motivated to such extreme levels that people think that there's 'something wrong with me'. Everything about me as a person – my health, my income, my contribution to society, my personality, my happiness have drastically improved because I have mastered the art of motivation through goal setting.

As you read the following chapters it is important that you follow the 4Wheel Drive Goal Setting Method for each area of your life. When you have a goal for each area of your life and you take action on them all every single day, you'll notice everything in your life start to improve.

Big Dreams = Big Motivation

"All our dreams can come true, if we have the courage to pursue them."
WALT DISNEY

Think of goals in 3 categories: 1-Goals you know you can achieve, 2-Goals you think you can achieve and 3-goals you actually *want* to achieve. Type 1 Goals and Type 2 goals create no leverage or inspiration for you. They are exactly the type of goals that mean you have to read this chapter on motivation. Type 3 Goals, however, inspire you to take **action**; they are so compelling that motivation is no longer an issue.

I'll give you an example; I used to have the goal of "being a life coach with 10 clients" (Type 1 Goal, I knew I could do this). I then had the goal of, "50 people have been through my life coaching program" (Type 2 Goal, I thought I could this). At the time of writing my goal is now; "to impact the lives of over 1,000,000 people globally through my books, products, seminars and speeches. (Type 3 Goal - This is what I really want!). I don't need any outside inspiration anymore. I know what I want, I truly **believe** that I can achieve it and I have no idea how to do it right now but that doesn't matter.

You Are Already a Master of Motivation!

You have already mastered motivation you just don't realise it. A true mastery of motivation comes from being 100% committed to something. Do you need to watch a motivational video or listen to motivational music to wash yourself every day? Of course not; you are just 100% committed to being clean and hygienic. You just do it! What if you had this same approach to doing whatever it is you currently 'wish' you were motivated to do?

It is absolutely crucial that you get in touch with what you are motivated to create in your life every day! This reprogramming process is amazing because I have realised over time that if you don't program yourself, you will be programmed by the environment and the people closest to you.

Do You Have a Big Enough Reason?

If you were in bed and you realised that your house was on fire would you roll over and have '5 more minutes sleep' or would you be MOTIVATED to jump out of bed and get yourself and your family to safety as quickly as possible? You would take immediate **action**, the REASON being that if you didn't, you and your family would probably get trapped and die.

The most important factor in being motivated to achieve anything is WHY? Different things act as motivators for different people but we all have certain things can get us to take action. With a bit of deep thought we can all come up with a compelling list of things to motivate ourselves. There are things like 'making a positive difference to the world', 'becoming financially free', and 'doing it for my family'. When these are all aligned you'll quickly realise that you won't ever have to worry about being motivated ever again because it is happening whether you feel motivated or not.

Stop and Write it Down

Pick something you want to achieve in your life and write down every reason you can think of as to why it HAS TO HAPPEN for you.

Now you can close your eyes and picture how the 100% committed version of yourself operates. Feel how great it feels to be constantly taking action on your goals. As you do this make sure you have a big smile on your face and notice how motivated you feel right now to finally make your life exactly how you want it to be.

Chasing Good Feelings & Escaping Bad Feelings

You know exactly what you want your ideal life to look like and yet you still don't take the action that would make it a reality. What keeps you from starting that new exercise regime? What stops you from acting on that business idea that you have had for as long as you can remember? Why haven't you started taking control of your finances?

You are 100% aware of the fact that taking these actions will improve your life on an *intellectual* level, so why don't you do it? It is because you believe that escaping the bad feelings associated with taking those actions is more important than the potential good feelings. What if you went through the physical pain and struggle of that difficult exercise regime only to put all the weight back on anyway? What if the business was a flop? What if you had to give up doing the things you love to do in order to sort your finances?

When I first encountered this idea, I became obsessed with the discovering why people who were obviously experiencing bad feelings would carry on living in exactly the same way. It became apparent that these people simply weren't experiencing bad feelings that were INTENSE ENOUGH to force them to make a change. If you have ever made a **decision** to finally lose weight, gain muscle or finally improve your health it was because you have so many intense bad feelings in association with how your body was looking you simply were not willing to live like it anymore. It is quite simple when you think about it like this. What motivated you? You wanted to escape the bad feelings that being out of shape brought into your life and you were chasing the good feelings that would come with looking and feeling good.

Understanding this linkage of seeking good feelings and avoiding bad feelings to our behaviour can help us be motivated to do anything we want, or indeed de-motivate us from doing the things that do not help us.

I remember my mother telling me the story of the time she thought it would be 'cool' to have a cigarette. At this time she was chasing the good feeling of being 'cool'. Fortunately for her, my grandfather caught her in the act and in his wisdom made her smoke the whole pack there and then. Although this may seem extreme it was certainly enough to make sure my mother never touched a cigarette ever again. For the rest of her life my mother has been escaping the INTENSE bad feelings of vomiting, difficulty breathing etc. that she had associated with smoking cigarettes.

Your life is about to totally change when you realise the power of this concept. The amazing thing about motivation is that you are clearly motivated to do some things in your life but these things may not help you and may have a direct impact on your motivation to do other things. For example if you are motivated to stay up late every night, it is likely that you are not going to be motivated to get up early in the morning. It is vitally important that you address the things that you are motivated to do but want to eliminate as well as increasing your motivation to do the things that you know will improve your life. I used to be very motivated to go out on the weekends and spend more money than I earned on alcohol. I was chasing the good feelings of feeling 'free', 'staying young', 'living for the moment' and many more. I was also trying to escape the bad feelings of 'being boring', 'stuck in a routine' and 'never enjoying myself'.

Stop and Write it Down

Think of something that you seem very motivated to do that you know isn't good for your health, wealth or long term happiness and write down the good feelings you are trying to create by doing it and the bad feelings that you escape. Keep writing; allow every feeling to hit the page.

Now write down all of the intense bad feelings that could potentially happen if you keep engaging in this behaviour. For example, I wrote down that I could: have a stroke/heart attack or any other alcohol induced illness, I would never fulfil my potential and die a 'nobody', I would be a disgrace to my family if I continued. Even as I write these words I am so grateful that I have escaped those bad feelings. You will too. Keep writing, let every feeling come out.

_____
_____
_____
_____
_____
_____
_____
_____
_____
_____

You can now pick something that you want to be motivated to do. Write down all of the amazing feelings that you will create for yourself by **taking this action** and write down all of the bad feelings you will be escaping. This will be twice as powerful if you can utilize the same feelings that you were chasing and escaping before. As an example, you'll remember that I wanted to feel like I was 'free', like I was 'staying young' and like I was 'living for the moment' and I didn't want to feel 'boring', 'stuck in a routine' and like I was 'never enjoying myself'. I have used these feelings to my advantage because I am now EXTREMELY motivated to be a global name in the field of personal development and travel the world, spreading my message. Why? Because I know that I'll feel 'free', 'young' and 'in the moment' as I live this lifestyle and I certainly won't find it 'boring', I won't be stuck in a routine and I'll certainly be 'enjoying myself'. Have some fun with this, write as much as you can and you'll notice how great it feels to realise you can get the same feelings and approach the life of your dreams at the same time.

_____
_____
_____
_____
_____
_____
_____
_____
_____
_____

Awareness and repetition are very important when comes to making this work for you. When you feel yourself wanting to break your new eating habits and just go on a binge be AWARE of the fact that you are just chasing a good feeling. Then stop and picture the pain of being overweight again and all of the illnesses that will come your way if you eat like this. It is about thinking about the long term feelings. Do you think as many Double Cheeseburgers would be eaten if three seconds after you ate one, you gained twenty pounds and had a heart attack?

That 'Little Voice' In Your Head

You go to bed motivated and totally ready for tomorrow. You 'know' that you are going to get up early, go to the gym and start the day with amazing momentum. You go to sleep safe in the knowledge that tomorrow is going to be a day full of motivation. The next morning your alarm goes off and you immediately hear words like "really?, it can't be time to get up already", " I'll hit snooze, 5 more minutes won't hurt", "I tell you what, you can start that new routine tomorrow" WHAT HAPPENED?!?!

That wasn't you speaking in that example; it was what I call, your 'little voice'. Your little voice can be a troublemaker, it does only want to protect you but it really can sabotage you and drain you of all your motivation, right on the spot! You probably hear that little voice in your head every day in so many different situations. "You can't do that", "that's too difficult"; "don't ask her on a date, she might say no". You may have even heard it as you've read this book, "that wouldn't work for me", "what is this nonsense?". It is trying to protect you through a fear of things going wrong if you try to improve and it knows that you are 'safe' where you are.

The most relaxing realisation that you can have is; this voice isn't you! It is your conditioned mind that may have been negatively programmed at some point or another. The chances are that it will always be there, but it is up to you how you respond to it and how you view it.

Think of something that your 'little voice' says to regularly; it'll be things like "You can never lose weight", "You can't start a business" and "you'll always be single". Hear it saying those words to you now, where in your head is it? What does it sound like? Is it speaking fast or slow? Loud or quiet? Now picture the same voice talking out of your belly button in a silly voice like Donald Duck or a Silly accent. Notice how you have control over it and realise it isn't as threatening now.

One of the most powerful things that I did when I was taking control of the conversation in my head was to visualize my 'little voice' and draw what he would look like, he turned out to be this tiny stick man with a speech bubble coming out of his mouth and scraggly hair. After I did this I realised that I had a 'Big voice' as well, the voice that tells *you can* do things and knows that it is your duty to create the best life possible even if it does mean some **persistence** and a few calculated risks. I then visualized my 'big voice' and in the true unpredictable fashion of the human mind it turned out to be champion Bodybuilder Kai Greene. If you don't know who Kai Greene is, he is a giant of a man with huge muscles in every area of his body. Now, if a battle takes place in my head between the "you can't" of the little voice and the "you can" of the big voice, Kai Greene is going to dominate a little stick man every day of the week!

Stop and Write it Down

Take the time to visualize and then draw what your little voice looks like with a speech bubble saying something it usually says to de-motivate you. Then visualize and draw your BIG VOICE with a bigger speech bubble; powerfully saying the opposite, motivating words.

Whenever you notice yourself feeling de-motivated by the things you are saying to yourself, have the **discipline** to realise that it isn't you and it is that harmless little drawing. **Visualize** your big voice taking control and motivating you to take **action.**

Be **persistent** with this and soon you will notice that your Big voice is running the show and you will be on a motivated fast track to achieving your goals. Which is what you want, right.

Motivation Is Just A Feeling

The interesting thing about motivation is it is just a feeling, like happiness or sadness. So it's important that you do that little bit extra, every day to create the *feeling* of motivation. I can't tell you what that is for you, but you will already know.

I like to watch motivational videos and I watch at least one every day, usually in the morning. Ones with inspirational music work the best because they invoke deeper feelings. The important thing is that you do exactly what makes *you* feel motivated at least once a day. Read over your 'WHY'S' every single day. If you have the type of job that allows you to personalize your work space then have motivational images and words everywhere you can. This will allow you to **focus** on motivational feelings and the **images in your mind** will be constantly inspirational.

Future Truth

"I am totally committed to creating the body, finances and life of my dreams. Success is inevitable for me because I always keep going"

[TAKE A BREAK]

BODY BEAUTIFUL – TRANSFORM YOUR BODY AND HEALTH

"Take care of your body. It's the only place you have to live." JIM ROHN

The greatest gift we have,
Is this miraculous human body
So why is it in modern times
We are treating health like a hobby?

No matter what you love,
Good health is just implied.
Without it, fun is difficult
Ask anyone who's died

I acknowledge the fact that
This isn't possible right now
But we can show respect for those we've lost
Let me tell you how

We can appreciate our bodies,
And be healthy, fit and strong
Or we'd be disrespecting our presence here
And that would just be wrong

Enjoy yourself, of course
But the man who has most treats
Is the man who is here the longest, by exercising and watching what he eats.

The Two Things Your Body Needs, Every Day

Oxygen and water are the two things that we NEED regularly to operate at our absolute best. The challenge in modern society is that we are increasingly becoming a culture of dehydrated, shallow breathers.

One dramatic turnaround that I made in my life was to take conscious control of my breathing and water intake. Three times per day I engage in deep breathing that highly oxygenates my body, removes toxins and helps to relieve any stress. All I do is breathe in deeply and count how many seconds I breathe in for, then I hold it for four times and as long and then I breathe out for half as long as I held it. For example, if I inhale for 4 seconds, I hold it for 16 seconds and then exhale for 8 seconds. I do this for 10 breaths and it feels amazing. It is particularly fantastic at removing that 'groggy' feeling first thing in the morning which is caused by shallow breathing during sleep.

I also carefully monitor my water intake and I aim to eat as many water rich foods and vegetable juices as possible. This is something you can do gradually, starting straight away. You can start by committing to making sure you drink 2 Litres+ of water per day (or whatever amount will keep you hydrated in the lifestyle you lead). You can then progress to adding some cucumber or celery to your diet. Then when you notice how great you feel, you can begin adding green juices to your lifestyle to feel even better.

I realise that the notion of green juice sounds crazy right now, and it would have to me, 3 years ago. I can only speak from personal experience and not the experience of anyone else but I have noticed dramatic improvements in my health, vitality, energy and physical appearance by drinking the juices of green fruits and vegetables like cucumber, celery, limes and kale.

Eating To Release Energy

The title of this chapter is 'Body Beautiful'; this is not simply meant in the sense of 'magazine cover' like bodies. I mean all of your internal organs working in harmony. I mean how beautiful it is to have your body in a position where it releases the energy required to do everything that you want to do in life.

I realized very early on that massive results needed massive energy and the way I was eating was making me tired and lethargic and activating my chronic asthma. You may be reading these words thinking "that's great, but how do I get an attractive looking body?" An attractive, *sexy* looking body takes care of itself if you are eating and exercising in a way that is optimal to your health and energy. It is then very simple to progress to enhancing specific areas of your body through targeted, muscle building exercises.

The amount of books that are dedicated to this topic probably number in the thousands and there are probably more being written and published right now. I read many of these when I was on my quest to cure myself of asthma and increase my energy levels to new heights. What I discovered was that a lot of theories of optimal diet contradicted each other. The only thing that made sense to me was to try everything and see what worked best for *me personally*. I will, of course be describing the things that we all 'know' to be beneficial like eating more green vegetables but the most important message is to find out what foods make you feel energized and not like you need to go to sleep thirty minutes later.

Exercise Is Fun When You Know How

The thing that I find amusing about exercise is that I don't have to tell you all of the benefits. You know you'll be happier, you know you'll be healthier, you know you'll look better. So why don't you do it every day?

Having just read the chapter on Massive Motivation you will have some clearer answers to this question. You are probably just attaching too many bad feelings to actually exercising and not enough bad feelings to not exercising. The chances are you are also letting your 'little voice' take control when the time comes to exercise and you say things like "I'll start tomorrow".

I'm not suggesting you compete in a triathlon (although that would be a fantastic goal); if you are not exercising regularly right now. Starting with a fifteen minute walk, cycle or swim would be amazing. The most important thing that you can do is **decide** that you are going to exercise every day and then have the **discipline** make it a **habit.** You can then build on this and there will be no shock to the system, you can build in variety and discover what type of exercise makes you feel the best. You can then build on this through the use of **goals.** You could aim to run the London Marathon in two years time and start by taking a fifteen minute walk around the block, tomorrow. With this goal in mind, you will gradually build up to running and then as time progresses, increase the distance.

Unfortunately, there is no secret sauce to this. Improving your eating habits and exercising regularly is what I believe to be the only sure-fire way to become healthier and happier with what you see in the mirror.

Jump For Joy!

I'd like to tell you a little bit about the wonder of the mini –trampoline or the 'rebounder'. When I first heard about this supposedly healthy past time, I thought that it was just fad but as you can probably tell by now, I love researching positive results. It turned out to be one of the greatest gifts that I could have given my body and I still continue to 'rebound' two years on. My research suggests that there are over 34 related health benefits to rebounding that are too plentiful to describe within the constraints of this book.

Stop and Write it Down

However, this book IS about rapidly turning your life around so there are some highly relevant benefits listed below and to help decide that a rebounder could be for you; you can write down why this benefit would improve your life.

Benefit: Can help to decrease stress.

This will be good for me because,

_____

_____

Benefit: Your ability to manage your BMI (body mass index) improves as well as your muscle to fat ratio.

This will be good for me because,

_____

_____

Benefit: If done in the morning your energy levels could be higher for the whole day.

This will be good for me because,
_____
_____

Benefit: Regular rebounding has been shown to decrease the breakdown of cells due to aging (you could look younger)

This will be good for me because,
_____
_____

Benefit: Regular rebounding has been shown to create deeper and more relaxed sleeps.

This will be good for me because,
_____
_____

Train Your Body to Burn Fat

Your body will not burn fat unless you make a conscious decision to train it to. At this point it is also vital to **believe** that you can get rid of that stubborn layer of fat around your abs. As long as you have the belief that it is possible and you can create an image in your mind of what you will look like with your new 'fat free' midsection then you can begin. It's a nice feeling to picture yourself with your dream body, isn't it.

Have you ever tried to take all of the fat out of your diet and then gone a step further by eating so much less that you feel hungry all the time? You probably then wanted to *escape this bad feeling* so you ended up eating exactly like you did before and put all of the weight back on and more? Your body panicked and became even better at storing fat for you than it was before.

Why not stop trying to 'lose weight' and **decide** to 'release' unwanted body fat? This serves wonderful physiological and psychological purposes. Physiologically you can make sure you are actually releasing unwanted fat and not valuable muscle or water and psychologically you have 'released' the weight rather than just 'lost' it. What is the first thing you try to do when you lose something? Exactly, you try to 'find it'; by *releasing* the weight you will be psychologically less likely to 'find it' again.

I have been asked in the past, how do I stay in such good shape when I eat so many Avocados; aren't they full of fat? They are full of fat but they are full of good fats, in fact Avocados are one of the most diversely beneficial foods that you could eat in whole world. My point is that it is important that you give your body sufficient good fats so that it can use it as fuel because if you starve your body of fat, it will store it.

Combine this with regular aerobic exercise, like running, cycling or swimming and you are literally beginning to train your body to burn fat and operate in a more efficient way. One great by-product of this is you'll be looking and feeling great! Which is want ultimately, isn't it.

Eat Less Without Even Trying

Recently, I discovered what I now call 'the miracle of coconut oil'. I have three teaspoons of coconut oil every day, without fail. I have personally found the health benefits amazing. One interesting benefit is that it can curb that 'boredom hunger' where you would normally have a bar of chocolate or bag of crisps just to stop the cravings. Research suggests that this may be related to the way that the fatty acids in coconut oil are metabolized, because the ketone bodies have an appetite reducing effect.

There are also many other potential health benefits that may be caused by regular coconut oil consumption, most of which I have noticed in my life already. Things like, increased energy, improved immune system, lower blood cholesterol and reduced abdominal fat to name a few.

Get The Knowledge Then Live the Lifestyle

It is crucial that you acquire the **knowledge** that is necessary for you optimize your health and then **act on it**. Without even realising it, you could be ruining your chances of high energy and the body of your dreams. For years my Barbadian grandmother was telling me that too much dairy was no good for me as an asthmatic and someone with so many allergies but did I stop? No. I had the knowledge but I wasn't acting on it. It wasn't until I started to acquire more knowledge and start acting on it that I really started to improve my health and body. I learned that, amongst many other things, excessive dairy consumption causes the body to produce more mucous and can be highly detrimental to people with allergies, respiratory disorders (like asthma) and regular cold sufferers. Now my dairy intake is limited to a small amount that's in certain supplements I take or monthly 'treats'.

You will always have the free choice to eat whatever you want, whenever you want and no one can tell you otherwise. I just think that it is my duty to help you become aware of some of things that have helped transform the health of so many people.

You may be thinking this is wonderful, but what about the beach body that I want? I can tell you right now that your beach body is inevitable if you start eating and exercising like someone who wants to live a long, full life as a starting point. Once you have done this you can then use **goals** that can drive you towards your ideal body dimensions. You are then back in the positive cycle of **deciding** what your body's going to look like, adopting the **beliefs** of someone who can get that body, acquiring the **knowledge** required to build that body, having a **positive outlook** during your training and **visualizing** your body the way you want it as if you have already done it. Underpin all that with **action** and your success is a matter of time, isn't it.

It is not easy to make the change to being healthy and looking fantastic but it is certainly simple. Either you're head will be full of *excuses* that you can remove and replace with *reasons* or you can hold onto your excuses and stay right where you are.

Treat Yourself

One thing that is truly liberating is when you realise that you are having that piece of cheese, that pizza or that glass of red wine a couple of times per month out of choice and not out of a destructive daily habit. I have a client, (who we will call Cassandra for the purposes of this book) who literally swapped coffee for fruit tea; added a nutritious breakfast and stopped drinking alcohol in the week and she lost ten pounds of unwanted body fat in less than four weeks, whilst maintaining her muscle and fluids. The point is Cassandra still enjoyed a glass of wine on the weekends but she was enjoying it as a conscious treat rather than blindly chasing a good feeling out of habit with alcohol as the vehicle.

Start Now!

In my experience the biggest obstacle for people when it comes to turning their health and body around is that they don't get started and they don't make a plan that they can stick to and take action on immediately. It's always "I can't start today because it's my dad's birthday next week", "I'll start when I've booked that holiday" or "I'll start next month". THE TIME WILL NEVER BE RIGHT; YOU HAVE TO MAKE IT THE RIGHT TIME!

Stop and Write it Down

If you want to, you can start turning your life and health around and improve your body right now. You can create a plan following the template below. Of course you don't have to but if you can't stop and plan it how do you expect to actually achieve it?

I _____**decide right now** to commit to achieving the health, vitality, energy and body of my dreams.

The most powerful belief I have about getting the health and body I want is:

This will be good for me because,

_____

_____

The daily health habits (Deep Breathing, Water, Exercise, etc.) I am excited to start are:

_____

_____

I am going to use (books, internet, professionals, doctors etc.)

_____
_____
_____
_____to acquire the knowledge
that I need personally to be as healthy as possible.

Draw a picture below of yourself with the body of your dreams, have some fun with this, you can keep it private and exaggerate parts if you like.

My Primary Health and Body Goal:

It is (insert date)_____ and I weigh_____ pounds with _____% body fat. I feel amazing to be in the shape of my life and I feel energized, vibrant and extremely proud of myself.

I will achieve the this goal because (BIG REASONS)

_____
_____
_____
_____
_____
_____
_____
_____

I am not willing to put off my health any longer; I am committed to taking **action** from today onwards.

Always consult your doctor before making any changes to your diet or starting a new exercise regime.

Future Truth

> ***"I have the health, body and energy of my dreams. I have a massive amount of energy that allows me to live a full successful life."***

[TAKE A BREAK]

TIME MASTERY – HOW TO GET 'ENOUGH HOURS IN A DAY'

"Time = life; therefore waste your time and waste your life, or master your time and master your life."
ALAN LAKEIN

Time is here and then it's gone

Darkness falls after the sun has shone

As you age it goes faster and faster

And seems to be even more difficult to master

Everybody wants a piece of your pie

But you never have enough and you don't know why?

The secret seems to be, don't spend time…invest it

That's sounds pretty great but here is the best bit

Invest your time wisely and start moving towards

A life full of freedom and fantastic rewards…

It is, of course widely accepted that time is our most precious resource. Therefore, how we use this resource that we are so lucky to have will have a huge impact on our happiness and success. I have spent my life having very different attitudes towards time. I started off by ignoring the issue all together, believing that I would never run out of it and I could just float through life believing that I would eventually have a great life. It is clear that I now do not believe that one can just stumble upon a great life, it, of course has to be created.

When I first decided to improve my life I became a workaholic, you probably know at least one of those types of people. There is never enough hours in a day for the workaholic; they eventually (like I did) get to a point where they realise that their health is suffering and they are not seeing their family as often as they would like, if at all.

Time Mastery

"You may delay, but time will not." BENJAMIN FRANKLIN

My aim is to be what I now call a 'Time Master'. Mastering time is the key to your overall success, happiness and fulfilment. When I say mastering time what I mean is allowing time for every aspect of your life. As a Time Master, you will be able to put in 14 hours to your business but only if that is what is absolutely required at the time.

In my quest to be a Time Master, I have found myself often getting more done in a 6 Hour work session than a 12 hour work session. How? By making sure I not only 'work hard' but I also 'work smart'. You can start working smart by delegating those tasks that can be done by other people, even if you are the only person in your business, you can hire a freelancer. You may be thinking, "I can't afford a freelancer". What if I told you can't afford NOT to hire a freelancer". Think about this for a moment, would it not be wise to pay a freelancer £100 to complete a task for you so your time could be freed up to work on a project that could potentially generate £3,000?

Finish Tomorrow, Today

During my study of the most successful people on the planet I discovered one profound but amazingly simple strategy. They were all planning everything that needed to be done tomorrow, the night before. I really started to run with this idea and I smile as I write these words because last night planned to 'Write the chapter on time mastery'.

Utilizing this skill allows you to **visualize** exactly how the next day is going to go amazingly well for you. The majesty of your subconscious mind will then begin to creatively map out solutions to any challenges that arise throughout the day. I'm sure you've also heard of the phrase 'hitting the ground running'; by planning your day the night before, you can do exactly that. By lunchtime you are way ahead of any competitors you may have because you didn't have to 'figure out' what you were going to do because it was *already done.*

Don't Finish Your 'To-Do-List'

In modern society we are surrounded by things that 'demand' our attention and that need to be dealt with because they are 'urgent'. The major challenge with this approach is our time is often taken up by things that are urgent rather than things that are important. After all, when that email pops through or you get a notification from social media; you have to check it straight away don't you? One powerful idea that I have utilized is not doing everything on my to-do-list. If I didn't get the chance to check my social media or watch my favourite program but I did make time to set up a potentially lucrative business meeting, write 10 pages of my next book and spend quality time with a family member, the day is a massive success.

Stop and Write it Down

Be very honest with yourself and write down everything that you commit time to every day. Everything from checking social media, to watching TV, to exercising, to making business calls, to serving customers. Whatever you give time to every day. Now **focus** on and underline the things that are most important in your life and **focus** on what makes the biggest difference to your success and happiness. **Decide** that you are no longer willing to let the other things on your list interfere with the most important items.

_____
_____
_____
_____
_____
_____
_____
_____
_____
_____

Just Say No!

I am still in the process of putting this aspect of time mastery in to practice every day. It is so easy to say yes to anything and everything that comes your way because you always want to be friendly and helpful. The unfortunate reality of saying yes to everything is we have to spend valuable time getting out of things we shouldn't have got ourselves into from the start.

The best technique I have found is to say "to be totally honest and up front with you, I can't right now but if anything changes I'll let you know straight away". This allows me to **focus** on the things that are most important to me and stops me from adding to an already carefully balanced list of activities.

Do The Same Amount in Half the Time

There are many situations when you could be successfully doing two things at once. You can get really creative with this and it actually becomes quite fun. I know that exercise will always be on my action plan for the day and I also know that listening to some educational material will be as well. All I do is listen to the audios whilst I'm exercising, easy. You may be committed to playing with your children every day and also want to find time to do some light exercise. Why not go play with a ball game with your children in a nearby park?

Have a think about where you can make this technique work in your life and the results can be wonderfully time saving.

It Will Take Longer Than You Think!

How many times have you allotted an hour for an activity and it has taken two? Whenever you are planning your days, weeks or months make sure to realise that things often take longer than you would think. Adopting this mindset ultimately saves you time and any unnecessary stress. Your productivity will start to plummet as you notice the clock ticking on and on and you realise that you are going to have to be 'playing catch up' with your to do list.

When you overestimate the time it will take to do every task on your to do list then the worst that can happen is that it will take as long as you have predicted but most likely you will be so relaxed in the knowledge that you have enough time that you will find yourself in the wonderful position of being 'ahead of schedule'.

Learn From the Best and Save Time

I had no idea how to write to book, how to market a book, how to structure a book, how to speak about a book…you get the idea. This book would have probably taken 3 years longer to create if I hadn't sought out the people at the top of my field, purchased their books and attended their seminars that explained how to execute the whole process. In effect, I would have 'wasted time'.

It is absolutely crucial that you find a **role model** and find out what they **did** to create their success. Whatever career or endeavour you are in there is someone who either got to the level that you want to get to or managed to find a way to leave that job and do what you ultimately want to do. Find these people, interview them, buy their books, and attend their courses because this investment of time and money in the short term will pay dividends in the rest of your life. You will save yourself, literally, years.

Future Truth

> *"I am master of time. There is always enough time for me. I always do just the right thing at just the right time. I am always in control"*

Part 2

LIFT YOUR LIFE

RELATIONSHIP MASTERY – START CARING AGAIN

"I want to be in a relationship where you telling me you love me is just a ceremonious validation of what you already show me." STEVE MARABOLI

Give as much love as you can
Each and every day
So when you're gone
You're loved ones are still touched by you in every single way

Your gift of love to someone else
Is also a gift to you
Because that feeling that you give
Will return, multiplied by two

Put out the fire of anger
With feelings of adulation
An argument will finish before it starts
And you'll be back to admiration

Remember that you love them,
Really show them that you care.
After all, why would you do things on your own
It's much more fun to share...

It would be great to be motivated, achieve lots of business success and become financially free but what if you had nobody to share it with? I have found that truly caring and understanding the people closest to me to be an invaluable skill. As you become more successful you will appreciate the time and effort you put in to your relationships. Relationships are like anything other aspect in life; if it is not going forwards the chances are it is going backwards. It is imperative that you become aware of the relationships in your life that you are neglecting. Think of every one of your relationships and think about what you have done over the last 30 days to add to that relationship and make it grow.

Don't Just Hear; Listen

Your ears are never closed, so you will always be able to hear what is being said but listening and *paying attention* with the **goal** of understanding what the other person is saying is a totally different skill. Actually listening involves maintaining eye contact, watching their body to see if they are becoming more uptight or more relaxed as they deliver their message. Listening involves repeating information back to the person to make sure you have 'got the message'. When you are listening properly you will not get immediately defensive if it is something that you interpret as a potential 'criticism' and you will learn to genuinely...

See It from Their Point of You

Whether it is your friend, mother, father, husband, wife, colleague or employee; taking the opportunity to see it from their point of view will be the greatest gift to the progress of that particular relationship. I'll give you an example; when I first **decided** that helping people transform their lives as a coach, speaker and author was my purpose in life, I had to leave what was a well paying job. What happened next was that a lot of the people closest to me started to question what I was doing and it was 'a great job' (which it was) and it is crazy to try and make a career out of something like this. I had one of two choices; either I could get very defensive and tell them they are wrong and let an argument take place. Or I could allow myself to see it from their point of view. When I did that, I had no bad feelings towards them whatsoever. Of course it seemed crazy. I had always wanted a well paying graduate job, I had beaten 900+ applicants to the post, I was doing extremely well and then I left after a short time. They would be crazy *not* to think I was crazy.

Seeing the situation from their point of view meant that I could calmly sit them down and explain that this was a **decision** that I had made and that I was going to be **persistent** in making it happen. I could sit down and explain that I loved them very much and would appreciate whatever support they could give me and I would do everything in my power to live my purpose and create the best life imaginable for me and for them.

Stop and Write it Down

There will be a situation in your life right now where you feel like someone 'doesn't understand you' or it feels like they are 'on your back' all the time. I want you to think about this situation (only pick one if there are a few) and I want you to pretend that you are the other person. Write down everything that they are feeling and how they are seeing the situation. You'll quickly notice that you feel better about the situation and realise that you have the power to improve the situation now that you see both sides.

_____

_____

They Can't Argue on Their Own

The dictionary definition of an *argument* is 'an exchange of diverging or opposite views, typically a heated or angry one'. The key word for me here is exchange. The word exchange means that two people have to be involved. If you remove yourself from the exchange of opposite views then it can't be an argument anymore. It doesn't matter whether it's your spouse or a work colleague; you can take control and turn the argument into a discussion where you can *see the situation through their eyes* and turn the argument into a discussion with an actual resolution at the end of it, rather than two angry people going nowhere.

B.P.T.R

I know that the above approach sounds great in theory but what **action** can you take to make it a reality. Whenever I can feel myself on the verge of what could potentially be an argument with someone I love or a peer I think to myself "come on Jermaine; B.P.T.R". B.P.T.R stands for Breathe, Pause, Think, and Respond. If you were totally honest with yourself; if you utilized this technique in the last 'argument' you had it wouldn't have happened. Most arguments escalate to the next level because you *react* and say something that ten minutes later you wish that you hadn't said. True or true? Do this yourself and you'll notice huge improvements with all of your interactions with other people and most importantly, those you love. Next time you find yourself in a situation where someone in your life says something that could create 'that feeling' where you just want to 'bite back'...BREATHE – take the oxygen in that will allow you think clearly. PAUSE - allow your conscious mind to take control. THINK – let the most useful resourceful, 'solution-focused' response come to you and only then should you RESPOND.

Intimate Love

With regards to intimate relationships I believe that it is important do exactly what you would have done at the start of the relationship, throughout the relationship and this makes it so much more likely that will never be an end to the relationship. If you would have randomly turned up with flowers on your fourth date make sure you randomly turn up with an even bigger bunch of flowers three years later. If you would have given them a massage for no reason when you first started seeing each other, give them a massage today.

Stop and Write it Down

Really sit back and allow all of the memories of the things that you used to do for your partner at the start of your relationship to come into your consciousness. Notice some of things that you no longer do or the things that you do 'once in a blue moon' and write them down so you can commit to regularly doing them again.

_____
_____
_____
_____
_____
_____
_____

Daily Love

It is probably becoming clear as you read this book that what you do day-to-day will ultimately impact your results. One area of life where it easy to neglect this principle is in our intimate relationships. We forget the 'little things' that make a big difference. There are genuinely so many things that you can do EVERY DAY that have little or zero financial cost that really can make your partner feel that extra bit more loved. Introduce daily passion into the mix as well and long-term success is inevitable.

Personally, I like to write what I call a 'little love note' every single day, with a message of love, appreciation and gratitude. If you just rolled your eyes or 'cringed' at the concept you probably could benefit from this more than most people. It is also crucial to make sure you make a 'big deal' out of the first time that you see your partner at the end of the day. Take your head out of the TV, your phone or your computer and jump up and give them a big passionate kiss. This may sound like an amazingly simple idea and I truly **believe** that it will make all of the difference for you.

Compliment Your Partner in Public

We seem to have developed into a culture in which it is acceptable to make derogatory 'jokes' about or our loved ones when we are around other people. How often do you hear the wife described as "the old ball and chain" or "the dragon" or something similar? How regularly do you notice your friends putting their partner down in a group setting and then everyone awkwardly laughs about it? DON'T GET INVOLVED! Talk about your partner like you love and admire them when they are around and when they are not around. This will create an amazing energy for you as a couple and your relationship will stand out as one that is growing and full of passion and connection.

Stop and Write it Down

Make a list of things that you know that you could do every day that wouldn't cost any money but would take your relationship to new levels of connection and love. Even if things are great for you, what else can you do make it *even better?*

Youd Need Goals

You have a goal for your body, you have a goal for your finances, you seem to have goal for every area of your life apart from what could arguably be the most important. Think about it; we have already established that for something to make progress and improve it has to be moving towards a worthy goal. In a relationship it is very easy to get 'comfortable', however, this is dangerous state to be in and what was once a beautiful relationship can begin to slide backwards. As with any part of our lives the easiest way to combat this is to **set a goal**. You could set a goal to take your partner on a weekend away or to buy them flowers once a month or take them for a meal once a week. What you do isn't as important as committing to actually doing something.

Stop and Write it Down

Set a relationship goal right now. What could you commit to achieving in your relationship that gets you excited because you know it will great for the both of you? [If you are not in an intimate relationship, then it is also important to have goals for your other relationships so you can use the below template for a different relationship in your life.]

It is (insert date) _____ and I feel amazing because I have _____ which has improved my relationship and I feel a deeper connection and passion for _____ than ever before .

Women Need to Vent

Women are biologically wired to connect and men are biologically wired to 'fix things'. This is absolutely fine and poses no challenges whatsoever as long as both parties understand how to deal with certain situations.

When a woman is going through her day and certain, negative things happen; it is like she a 'post it note' stuck to her with a little description of what happened in that given situation. By the end of the day she may be covered head to toe in these post it notes saying things like; "Sandra gave me a dirty look at work today", "I can't believe how disgusting that lunch was" and "I forgot my gym clothes so I couldn't workout".

If a man's wife, girlfriend, mother or sister ingested some chicken that he noticed was still raw in the middle what would he immediately want to help her do? He'd want to help her to 'get it out' as quickly as possible through vomiting or laxatives etc. because the bacteria in the raw chicken is going to cause her pain and discomfort if it stays inside of her.

The fascinating about when the women in our life want to share all of the 'bacteria of life' they have picked up throughout the day and get it 'off their chest' we (as men) try to 'fix things' straight away. What we are doing here is stopping the 'emotional bacteria' from coming out and we are almost trying to force some back in. The real trick here to allow the women in our life to 'get it ALL out' and all we have to do is LISTEN. If she says "will you help me do something about this?" *then* offer some thoughts on solutions.

If all of 'this emotional bacteria' is allowed to build up then she'll start to hate the way she feels and start to feel truly down. It can then get to a point where the 'eruption' of emotional bacteria is going to be explosive and it's going to be difficult to deal with. The secret is to allow her to empty herself of the negative, emotional bacteria every single day because then you will only be collecting a little bit at a time. One successful technique for women to employ in these scenarios is to say something like "Honey, I've had a crazy day and I need to get some stuff off my chest. I don't need you to do anything I'd just love it if you could listen. Would that be okay?"

Finding The Person of Your Dreams

To find who you are looking for you need to know who you are looking for. This might sound simple but a lot of people don't find the person of their dreams because they simply don't know what this person is like. If you don't know exactly what it is you are looking for in a man or woman then how is your mind supposed to send you a green light when you meet someone that could be an amazing person for you to spend the rest of your life with?

Stop and Write it Down

You stand much more of a chance of finding a partner for life if you take the time to design what they look like, how they smile, what they do, how positive they are, what their hobbies are and places they'd like to go. Have fun right now and design your perfect partner. [If you already have the person of your dreams, you can write down all of the attributes that they have that you are truly grateful for and you will also feel amazing.]

_____

_____

_____

Future Truth

> "I am dedicated to constantly improving every relationship in my life. I give love, care and attention to all of my loved ones and the more love I give, the more I feel loved"

[TAKE A BREAK]

THE 'RAT RACE' – DO WHAT YOU LOVE OR LOVE WHAT YOU DO.

"Whatever your life's work is, do it well. A person should do their job so well that the living, the dead, and the unborn could do it no better."

MARTIN LUTHER KING, JR.

I had a friend who's biggest hate,
Was the first day of the week.
Over time I realised
This wasn't really unique

Most people I speak to,
Have this Monday based affliction
The strange thing is they wanted the job
Is this not a contradiction?

I hate my job, it gets me down
Is what I often hear
"So why not starting taking steps,
To escape the pain and drear?"

"I don't know what to do?!?"
Nor does anyone when they start,
It's their passion, belief and drive,
That truly sets them apart.

By following your passion,
And making life less bleak.
You'll be truly on the road to loving every day of the week...

If you are anything like me when I first committed to improving every area of my life, you probably have a job and you have a passion but they are not the same thing. Throughout University and for a short period after, I did many different jobs that I certainly wasn't passionate about but, of course, I 'needed the money'. The best advice I have is to continue to make the money you need from your current job, whilst getting in touch with what you enjoy about your job (if you had to) and working part time on your passion and your fortune.

Can I Really Love My Job?

Anything that does not bring you joy or happiness for a long period of time usually means that it is time to make a change. When it comes to your job, this does not necessarily mean that you have to leave it. You know that right now the job is giving you the money that you need so it is intelligent to remain in the job, so what you need to do is get out the 'rut' you are in and *learn* how to love your job.

Progress & Challenges

How can you make progress in your job? Is there a promotion available at some point in the future? If there isn't ask for more responsibilities so that you are always learning new skills until eventually they will have to pay you more for what you are doing.

It is very easy to get lost in the 'boring' things you do every day and convince yourself that you don't want to do anything else on top of those things. However, you can easily set yourself little targets and challenges by doing more than you are paid for and you will start to feel excited again. This is true of any job; I know because I have lived it. For many years I was a labourer for a property maintenance company and I started to feel like 'a chimp could do my job'. I then played a game with myself, could I become so resourceful, so productive and ahead of schedule that the tradesman would 'notice' if I wasn't there? I started making sure that everything was ready for the next phase of every job. I would love how one of my bosses would ask me for something and it would already be waiting behind them. I wasn't being paid to take this level of care with my job (nowhere near it) but it made my life so much more fulfilling and the job that much more enjoyable.

Stop and Write it Down

Write down some things that you could start doing that would be a challenge for you; things that you are not paid to do. Then visualize yourself doing them and notice how you immediately feel better about yourself and your job. 74% of people actually do this exercise so well they are excited to go to work and try it out as soon as possible!

_____
_____
_____
_____
_____
_____
_____
_____
_____
_____

You Are Important

Whatever you do for a job and however you have been feeling about it recently, you have to recognize the fact that your job is important otherwise it wouldn't exist. Be proud of whatever you do and take the time to recognise the value that you bring right now. Whose life do you make easier? How do you serve the greater good? How do you serve the public? Ask these powerful questions and you will start to get great answers.

If You Don't Like It, Do It First.

Successful author and entrepreneur, Brian Tracy, has a phrase "eat the frog"; which means to do the things that are going to be the most challenging, boring or both right at the start of your working day. As the day progresses, your day will get gradually more 'fun' and you won't be spending your day 'dreading' those things that you don't want to do.

What If You Were About to Lose It?

Have you noticed that whenever someone is about to lose something; whether it's a house, a car or job it becomes immediately more valuable to them. This is because all of the reasons why they *want and need it* come racing the front of their minds.

Stop and Write it Down

It's time to complete the sentence "I like my job because…" as many times as you can. Your initial reaction could be "I don't like anything about my job and I don't like the people either". That's fine but are you working there for free? Probably not. Do you LIKE the fact they pay you? Of course you do; so your first sentence will be **"I like my job because.. *they pay me*"**. Once you have the first one you will notice more start to flow and how obvious they are: paid holidays? A pension? A parking space? A canteen with good food? Do you live close? Do not carry on reading until you have completed every sentence.

I like my job because
_____

I like my job because
_____

I like my job because
_____

I like my job because
_____

I like my job because
_____

I like my job because
_____

I like my job because
_____

I like my job because
_____

I like my job because
_____

I like my job because
_____

I like my job because

_____

I like my job because

_____

Now you have completed every single one of the above sentences it will be amazing if you can stand up and read them just before you go to bed tonight and when you wake up in the morning. It is important not to just say them but you have to feel the emotion of them. If you like your job because they pay you and that means you can provide for your family. THAT IS AMAZING. Focus on the FEELING of self-worth that goes along with that. Do this every morning and night until you are totally refocused on seeing the good things about your job and not the old bad things that don't exist anymore.

Surround Yourself with Positive People

"Surround yourself with only people who are going to lift you higher."
OPRAH WINFREY

I should probably put this subtitle in every single chapter of the book because it makes such a huge difference to the quality of your life. It will be very difficult for you to create the new thought pattern of "I like my job" if you are surrounded by people that are constantly talking about how difficult life is and how much they hate their job. Give yourself the gift of spending time with people who are positive about their jobs and view them as a stepping towards bettering themselves so they can get to the lifestyle that they truly desire.

Part Time Passion

Take some to realise the things that you are passionate about in life. Make **the picture in your mind** of how amazing it would be to be doing it as a full time job. What do you see? What do you hear? What do you taste? What do you smell? How do you feel? Really get involved with the image in your mind as you start to feel your passion increase. Whether it is helping children, speaking, writing, cooking or making clothes; ask yourself is there someone in the world making a full-time living from doing this thing that you love to do? The answer will most probably be yes and the people at the top of your chosen passion will be very handsomely rewarded for their efforts. I came across a woman who was making six figures per year from teaching people how to knit!

The question is never; "is it possible?" The question is always; "am I willing to do what it takes to make it a reality in my life?" As long as the answer to that question is "YES" then you are in motion. Could you commit ten hours per week to starting a career for yourself in an area that you are truly passionate about? The important thing is to start!

For me personally, I started offering free coaching on the weekends so that I could hone my skills and work out what I could do to help people as quickly as possible. Then I started to educate myself for two hours per day on how to be a coach, an author and a speaker. Over time I started to do exactly what my **role models** had done to get to where they wanted to get to so that I could walk the same path. The very process I went through to get this book off the ground was simply the exact same process that one of my role models had been through.

I_____**decide right now** to commit to being in a position where my primary source of income comes from _____, something that I am truly passionate about doing every day.

The most powerful belief I have about achieving my dream career is
_____
_____
_____

My heroes in the area of my dream career that I am going to learn from are:
_____
_____
_____

The daily habits that will contribute to me gaining more skills and experience in relation to my passion are:
_____
_____
_____
_____
_____
_____
_____
_____

I am going to use (books, internet, professionals, doctors etc.)

_____

_____

_____to acquire the knowledge that I need have my dream career.

Future Truth

"I am so happy and grateful that I am working on my passion every day. I am proud to say that my primary source of income comes from my passion and I love every minute of it!"

There Is No Magic Pill

If it was easy to have something you are passionate about as your job then everyone would be doing it. However, as you have you have been reading this book, you have become acutely aware of the value of **persistence.** Depending on your beliefs, the chances are you only live once and I would love for you to live it doing something that you are passionate about, whilst making money and making a difference.

You have to be **persistent** with this, learn as often and as much as you can, and hold on to the **picture** of yourself working in your dream career on the screen of your mind every day. Find the **role models, take the action** and if it doesn't work, learn from it and **take new action.**

Build A 'Dream Team'

"Surround yourself with people who are smarter than you." Russell Simmons

At the time of writing, I am not exactly where I want to be just yet. I haven't spoken for 'Success Resources' or held a seminar for over 1000 people but here's the thing: **I know I will and I surround myself with people who believe I will and I spend time with people who are also chasing their passions.** It doesn't matter what a person is doing at this present time, if they have a compelling **vision** of the future like you do then you can join together for the ride. Celebrate each other's successes and pull each other back up after temporary defeat.

Join forums, networking websites, breakfast clubs and attend seminars. I promise you there is a group of people who are just as passionate as you are about improving their life and operating day to day within their field of passion. Seek out these people; it's not difficult in the world we live in today, a simple internet search could be all it takes. Will it be scary to jump in and go and meet new people like this? Probably. Should you do it anyway? Of course! I have met so many people that have been able to elevate me closer to my dreams just by attending various different events and community websites. Any apprehension that you feel is good because you are breaking free into something new and it means that you are well and truly on your way to a career that you love. The steps may not be easy but they'll certainly be simple. Especially if you manage your mind using what you have learned so far and manage the money from your current job in the way you're about to learn…

MONEY TROUBLES – THE MONEY SECRETS YOU WEREN'T TOLD IN SCHOOL

Part 1- A Money Mindset

"Money may not buy happiness, but I'd rather cry in a Jaguar than on a bus." – FRANCOISE SAGAN

We have already established that MONEY WILL NOT MAKE YOU HAPPY, which is absolutely fine because that was never its purpose. Money is just tool that will allow you to live the life of prosperity and benevolence you deserve.

Money will only make you more of **what you already are**. If you are sensible, friendly and charitable then you will become more so. If you are mean, reckless and thoughtless then these attributes will also become amplified.

One trick that really changed my life is to think of people in my life that I wouldn't exchange for £1,000,000 and I would already 'feel' wealthy. Do it now, **picture in your mind** those people that you would never dream of swapping for £1,000,000 and notice how amazingly wealthy you feel. You are already a millionaire just not in a monetary sense *yet*.

Money Matters

How often do you hear statements like "Money isn't everything" or "It's only money" or "Money doesn't mean much to me"? The fact of the matter is money matters! I am not saying that money is more important as anything else; I am just saying that it is sensible to recognize it as important.

Years Of Research

After I had taken care of my happiness, health, relationships and motivation I became obsessed with studying the differences between rich people and poor people. I read the books, attended the seminars and analyzed the teachings. My discoveries have been plentiful and have come from very practical, scientific teachers as well as what you might call 'spiritual' teachers. The thing that has fascinated me is the fact that they are all pretty much saying exactly the same thing – to become rich: you have to **think like a rich person thinks so you can then act like a rich person acts.** That might sound simple and even a little obvious but what are you going to do about it?

I have understood the concept for quite some time but I have only recently started **putting things into practice** and so many great things have started to happen. I always make the same joke to my friends; "I should have started with money and then improved my health and happiness". The point I am trying to make is that there are certain principles and practices that you can engage in that will allow you to make more money from various different sources after a relatively short period of time.

I have come to realise the importance of *repetition.* The ultimate success of things that I will be discussing in this chapter and probably every other idea in the book are based on the premise that you will stay **persistent** and repeat the ideas to yourself over and over again with the appropriate emotion. Think of it like reprogramming your 'mind software'. I bet that you can remember updating your smartphone recently, can't you. When the last time you updated the software in your mind?

From a psychological standpoint, your financial situation is a result of your 'past programming'. This is something that I really struggled with at the beginning of my journey; for many reasons I ended up being 'programmed' to believe that it was okay to go through life with the bank balance at zero and using credit cards to pay for everything that I wanted. It is only through rigorous repetition that I have now started to turn this around. In my first month of formal coaching I made five times more money in a month than I had ever earned and just a month later it was all gone.

How is it that eighty per cent of all lottery winners end up back where they were or worse off just five years later? The answer is that something must be happening in their minds.

Become Aware of The Abundance

> *"Abundance is not something we acquire. It is something we tune into."*
> **WAYNE DYER**

It is pretty obvious that you can only benefit from things that you are consciously aware of. For example, I would not be able to benefit from the speed and luxury of an aeroplane when I wanted to go and visit my family in Barbados if the Wright Brothers (and others) hadn't become consciously aware of 'the possibility of flight'. You have to agree, that everything you see around you (including this book) began as a thought in someone's mind, didn't it.

There is abundance all around us, the Giant Redwood has no limitations; it grows to its full, majestic height because that's 'just the way it is'. If you are like me and many other people who turned their finances around you probably need to address the level of conscious awareness of the potential money, wealth and abundance that is open to us all. Once you have done this you can begin to hold an **image in your mind** of what being financially rich would be like for you.

Stop and Write it Down

This next process changed my life because once I had written down and seen it on the screen of mind it felt more possible all of a sudden. **Write down and then visualize what life would be like if you were financially free. How you would you know? What do you see? What do you hear? What are you thinking? What do you smell? What would you taste? How amazing do you feel? Write down everything and then visualize it in big, bright, bold pictures and hold it in your mind as long as you can.**

The above task is one of those things that you can do anywhere. Once you have done it a few times you will be able to make yourself feel good and **believe** in yourself in the blink of an eye, just by returning to this vision.

Focus On Money

If you wanted to stop off and pick up a bunch of bananas on your way home from work, you would specifically **focus** on bananas and you would have a picture of bananas in your mind (like you do right now), you would go to the place in the shop where they would most likely be and go and get them, wouldn't you. Why don't we do that with money? One reason is because we don't focus specifically focus on the amount of money that we truly want. How often do you hear people say "I want more money"? The truth is I could transfer 1 penny into these people's bank accounts and their wish would have been granted; they'd have more money.

A principle that has been mentioned both deliberately and subconsciously in this book is the idea that *what you focus on expands.* Over the last few years I have found this to be especially true when it comes to money. If you focus on debt and never having enough money then that is what you get more of. If you focus on the things that you already have and the abundance that is already in your life then that is what you will get more of. This is the real reason why SOME of the 'rich get richer' and SOME of the 'poor get poorer' and NOT, contrary to popular belief because 'it takes money to make money' - remember those lottery winners who lost all their money?

Money will always come your way in some way shape or form and you need to condition yourself to be ecstatic every time it does. Do you pick up a penny that you see on the ground? Next time, pick it up and really *feel* grateful that some unknown source is sending you money and you will begin developing what is often referred to as a 'prosperity consciousness'. It would be amazing if every lost penny from around the world went directly into your bank account, wouldn't it.

Future Truth

> "*Amazing opportunities to make more and more money come my way every day*"

Money Mind Pictures

Our mind is a visual instrument; remember the bananas? Of course you do. The reason that you now see bananas in your mind's eye is the same reason as why you *now see a zebra with its black and white stripes*. The reason you 'see' the things that you think about is because that's how the mind works and you can very quickly change how you feel as well as the success you are attracting to yourself at any given moment by mastering this concept.

Stop and Write it Down

You're about to have fun realising the exact level of control you have over the pictures in your mind. Write down 10 random things (e.g. Cat, Hammer, Pen etc.) and then go back through the list and flick through a picture of each one in your mind like you were flicking through a child's picture book.

_____
_____
_____

Amazing, isn't it. But what does all of this picture business have to do with money? Think about an idea that we have already discussed: everything first begins as a thought and if a thought is an image then everything first begins with an image, doesn't it.

When humans became dissatisfied with windows being covered with animal hide, cloth or wood they built an image in their mind of being sheltered from the elements but also having the ability to see the outside world. The very moment the image was built in their minds and they decided to **take action** on it, what we now know as the glass window was inevitable. The same is true of your financial freedom, build the image in your mind and take action on it and it is inevitable (as long your **persistent** and prepared to **change your strategy**).

What Do You Believe?

Take a moment and think of your mind like a garden. Like any garden there are weeds. In this particular garden of wealth the weeds are strangling any possibility of the 'flowers of financial freedom' to grow. The weeds are all the beliefs about money that you have developed over the years that do not help you become wealthy. They are things that you have heard and learned that you have internalized as 'beliefs'. It's time to rip out those weeds right now and regain control of your own financial destiny. Circle some of the statements below that you have heard before reading this book:

"Money is the root of all evil"

"Money doesn't grow on trees"

"Not everyone can be rich"

"You need money to make money"

"Rich people are bad"

"Rich people are selfish"

"Rich people are only interested in money"

"It's only money"

These ideas that we receive early on in our lives can subconsciously ruin any conscious attempts we make at becoming wealthy.

Stop and Write it Down

What do you think of when you think about what your parents, grandparents, teachers, friends, colleagues and religious workers told you about money when you were a child and a young adult?

_____
_____
_____
_____
_____
_____
_____
_____
_____
_____
_____
_____
_____

Now go through everything that you may have lodged in your subconscious mind as a limiting belief and write them down again, only this time write as many positive, amusing, crazy opposites as you can underneath them. For example, underneath "Rich people are bad" you could write "Rich people are amazing, charitable and keep the country going with all of their taxes".

_____
_____
_____
_____
_____
_____
_____
_____
_____
_____

Future Truth

Now you have what I call 'flipped your beliefs on their head'. Make a conscious, deliberate, determined effort to say the new positive beliefs to yourself at least twice per day with energy and passion and financial freedom flowers will replace the poverty weeds in your 'wealth garden'.

[TAKE A BREAK]

PART 2 – MONEY MASTERY

"The art is not in making money, but in keeping it."
Proverb

Once you have become aware of the fact that our financial results are merely a 'printout' of what's going on inside your head then you can really start to implement some age-old techniques that will almost guarantee you long term wealth and enhance your short term security.

The First Part of Your Money Is……. Your Money!

I read the concept of 'paying myself first' many times before I started to implement it and realise its power because I was still battling my old programming. I'm predicting that because you have successfully got to part 2 of this chapter that you have come to terms with the idea of 'programming' at this point.

Think about this for a moment, money arrives in your account every month and then probably automatically starts to leave. Your mobile phone provider, your mortgage provider, your landlord, your gas provider, your electricity provider, a supermarket….the list goes on. Then you MAY keep some for yourself. Over the years I have realised that rich people do things slightly differently. Rich people keep 10%+ for themselves and depending on the type of system they follow they save it and never touch it or they invest it in something they have a great **knowledge** of. I have started doing this and now so should you. Why? *Because that's what rich people do!*

You may have read about several different 'money management' systems but this idea is present in them all. If you're like me, you may be thinking

"I can't afford to take 10% out before I even start!" The honest answer is your spending will adjust accordingly after you have paid yourself.

My Favourite System

Next comes what I call my "Ten Per Cent'ers" based on some of the ideas presented by one of my idols, T. Harv Eker in his book *Secrets of the Millionaire Mind*. I put ten per cent of every penny I earn into funding each of the following areas: ***Learning*** (Rich People commit to perpetually educating themselves in their area of business), ***Future Spending*** for things like watches, cars, holidays, etc. ***Fun & Treats*** is the ten per cent of my money I spend on things like extravagant evenings out or full massage treatments; every month.

The first time I encountered this concept was again in the inspirational book by T. Harv Eker in his book *Secrets of the Millionaire Mind* (I would also highly recommend attending his company's amazing course; *The Millionaire Mind Intensive*). I also create a feeling of balance in my life by using five percent of the money I earn to go towards my charity work. In the early months when I couldn't even spare the five per cent (although in hindsight I could have) I used to simply donate my time as opposed to the money and in many ways the gift of time to charitable causes is an even bigger one than money.

The remaining fifty five or sixty per cent goes into my *Daily Living Account* that pays for everyday needs like, rent, bills, food etc.

In my *Daily Living Account* my 'debt repayment system' kicks in. I was a student and a compulsive spender for a long time and this meant that I had debts to pay off. The absolute best way to do this was to make a plan, stick to it and send that money every month to pay off the debt and then spend the rest of my time **thinking about income** so I wasn't focussing on 'debt' (what you focus on expands, remember).

Money, Money, Everywhere!

What would it be like to be making money from 3, 4, 5 or 10 different sources whilst you were asleep? Think of your favourite celebrity and I can assure you that they do not make money from only one source and the chances are they do certain things (like release a song) and then get paid handsomely for it for many years after. At this point I must be clear that I know that we all may not be able to make money whilst we sleep through the same channels as Beyonce or David Beckham. However, we can all still make money whilst we sleep. I believe that we should all be striving to be in a position where we are working because we choose to, not because we have to for financial reasons.

There are many, many techniques to making this a reality in your life but it would take ten books to go into them all. However, there are several amazing books, courses and seminars in the 'Recommended Resources' section at the back of the book.

My research suggests that it doesn't matter what avenue you choose (Trading & Investing, Internet Marketing, Internet Business, Property Portfolios, Network Marketing etc.) but what does matter is the making of the **decision** that you want to create multiple streams of passive income for yourself and then learning about how to become proficient at it and then DOING IT! What I *can* say though, there is nothing quite like the thrill of the first time you make money whilst you're asleep or walking around the shops with your partner.

Future Truth

"I make huge amounts of money no matter what I am doing. I make money when I work, play and sleep. I make money 24 hours a day."

You Can Only Fail If You Stop

"Life is like riding a bicycle. To keep your balance you must keep moving." ALBERT EINSTEIN

When it comes to creating financial freedom, it is inevitably going to take a commitment to learning and **persistence**. However, you have the same **physiology** and **mental faculties** of all of the millionaires and billionaires out there and you can *and will* create the financial life you want for yourself. I am not there yet myself and I am implementing all of the above techniques every single day and at the time of writing I am poised to make more money this month than I ever have in a whole year! I don't tell you that to impress you I just mention it to impress upon you that when you **persist** in the techniques described above and follow some simple passive income strategies (see 'Recommended Resources' section) then you can make it happen.

Part 3

LIFT YOUR DESTINY

Build the New you – It's Time to Live by Design

"Open your eyes, look within. Are you satisfied with the life you're living?" BOB MARLEY

Why Are You Here?

When I first started to turn my life around I realised that I had to become the best version of myself along the way. I had to begin to truly get in touch with who I was, why I was here, and what my priorities were. This chapter will allow you to answer those questions for yourself. This process will involve the most writing because they really are about imprinting *the essence of you* and your future on to your subconscious mind.

I started with "Why am I here?" and this is what I came up with (I include my version of why *I* am here to show you how in depth and dramatic you can go with this). I wanted it to be from the heart and be filled with passion and I hope by reading mine you will write yours in the same way.

[Why am I Here? By Jermaine Harris]

I am here to humbly serve humanity by being a passionate example of the unlimited possibilities that life offers.

I am here to sincerely love everything in the universe and appreciate the miracle that is everything as well as every moment.

I am here to live life to the fullest because my life has a meaning and a purpose and to honour this is the most powerful way to show my respect

for myself and for my place in the universe by endeavouring to become more myself so I can set up strong example of what's possible for others because I believe that you only have one life and you have to enjoy the process.

I believe that you get what you give in life, so it is important to give everything and have a passionate love affair with myself to ensure that I have more to give because I want to reflect outward the gratitude I feel inside every single day. I make sure that my friends, family and loved ones are absolutely certain of my love for them.

I am here to feel excited about my life and what I can give, share and experience.

I am here to have an amazing time, create an unbelievable and inspirational story and leave behind a legacy that grows and inspires my friends and family for generations to come. I am here for those Magic Moments. I am here to Live Life on my terms. I will never settle for less than I can be, do create or give.

I am here to be a living example of the endless possibilities of humanity. I am here to be an inspiration to others. I am here to be a role model. I am here to be remembered and leave a legacy. I am here to be a leader. I am here to create a financial situation where I have the freedom to do what I want, when I want. So I can travel the world. So I can live my perfect day. I am here to live beyond 100 years of age. I am here for Health, Wealth, and excitement. I am here for big smiles, to be playful, to be inspirational and to be energetic

Stop and Write it Down

After just reading mine you've noticed how your mind has started to tell you why *you* are here and the reasons behind why you do what do, haven't you. Write them ALL down now. Include everything. WHY ARE YOU HERE?

_____
_____
_____
_____
_____
_____
_____
_____
_____
_____
_____
_____
_____
_____
_____
_____
_____
_____
_____
_____

I read the reasons why I'm here every other day to keep them front and centre of my mind. You will be doing something similar as part of the final chapter in 'The 30 Days that Change your Life".

What Comes First?

My day to day life has become a lot easier since identified what my priorities are and **put them in the order that made the most sense for my ultimate success and happiness.** To illustrate what I mean, here are my priorities in order:

1. Health, Wellbeing and High Energy Levels
2. Family and Love
3. Laughter
4. Gratitude
5. Self Education
6. Growth
7. Passion
8. Humility
9. Achieving
10. Investing
11. Contributing

Most people say at this point, "Surely family should be first?" And I would have said the same thing until I realised that if I didn't have my health and wellbeing then I wouldn't be alive or in a fit state to spend time with and look after my family anyway.

The wonderful thing about having an order as opposed to a list of things that are important to you is that there is never any conflict of interests and it doesn't take long to make a decision. For example, let's say I have the opportunity to speak to 5,000 people that could mean a large payday and a big 'achievement' but my Mum is taken ill all of a sudden and needs to go to the hospital; because I know that family is above achievement in my priorities I take my mum straight to the hospital. I know that this is an extreme example but you'd be surprised with the conflict that people have in these situations. You have probably heard people say "get your priorities straight"; this is the real life application of that phrase.

Stop and Write it Down

Write down your priorities in the order that *means the most to you* and consider the order carefully when thinking about your ultimate success and happiness making sure you don't have two things next to each other that are potential contradictions. There is no right or wrong order it has to mean the most to YOU.

_____

_____

_____

_____

_____

_____

_____

Who Are You?

I knew that I had big dreams and I knew that I wanted to do great things. However, *who I was* at the time could never make those things a reality. I had to create a vision of myself where I kept my true core and make sure that it lived up to the best version of Jermaine Harris humanly possible. I even included things that at the time were perhaps not strictly 'true' however; this gave me room to grow into this version of myself.

Once again, you may view this as a 'crazy' thing to do and I can assure you that all successful/fulfilled people are fully aware of who they are and who they are becoming. As with the 'Why am I here?' example I have included *my* answer to the question "Who am I?" that I remind myself of every other day. Remember that I have written this as a view of my ultimate self not through what may be perceived to over-confidence.

[Who am I? by Jermaine Harris]

I'm an extraordinary, passionate and loving man who loves people, family, friends, animals, changing lives & ideas that make a difference.

I love to discover and be creative. I love nature, beaches, beautiful scenery, travel, adventure, oceans, rivers, mountains, lakes, sunshine, wildlife and breathtaking views. I am a passionate man who takes the good things in life and makes them phenomenal and loves to share them openly, lovingly, passionately and playfully with others. I'm a massive source of inspiration. I'm a man with exceptionally high standards and excellent daily habits.

I'm a creator of possibilities, options, solutions, choices, opportunities and visions. I'm a creator of fun and laughter. I'm a creator of breakthrough moments. I'm an example of what's possible. I'm an amazing, boyfriend, friend, son, grandson, nephew, mentor, strategist, personal transformation coach, internet marketer, public speaker, entrepreneur, student, teacher, author, visionary and strategic planner.

I'm fun, I'm silly, and I'm playful. I'm outrageous, I'm adventurous and spontaneous.

I test the realms of possibility. I'm happy and fulfilled. I'm and athlete. I'm an author. I'm a great golfer. I'm a playful kid who can make anyone smile. I'm confident. I'm powerful I'm masculine. I'm attractive and handsome. I'm at one with the universe. I'm a leader. I'm a great listener, I'm a master communicator. I'm committed. I'm patient.

Stop and Write it Down

Write your fullest answer to the question "Who am I?" Consider it from the viewpoint of who are at your core mixed with the absolute best version of yourself that you can imagine. Notice how much fun you have with this just like I did.

_____
_____
_____
_____
_____
_____
_____
_____

[TAKE A BREAK]

Your Fantastic Future – Your Exciting New Journey

"Change is the law of life. And those who look only to the past or present are certain to miss the future." JOHN F. KENNEDY

I often get asked how do I get up so early some mornings and keep going all day? When you are enjoying the present moment and you are convinced that tomorrow is going to be even better; is there really any other way to live? The process described below is the most fun, imaginative, transformational experience I have ever gone through. It is the process that opened up all new possibilities for me and helped to realise that many people have already done the things that I want to do, so by definition they are possible.

Silence The Little Voice

Remember the exercise we did where our 'BIG' voice silenced our little voice; it's time to be prepared to do just that. The minute that you start creating all of these amazing **visions** of the future your little voice is going to start saying things like "how the hell are *you* going to achieve something like that?"

So be excited now, be bold, remove any limitations and design the future that you want for yourself because if you don't, who will?

DESIGN YOUR DREAM DAY

Stop and Write it Down

Already stored in your subconscious mind is the script for your ideal day. As you read that you'll notice that an **image** of this day is starting to come to the surface. What does your ideal day look like? What do you do all day? Who are you with? How do you feel? Write it all down right now, remember this is your *ideal* day; money is of no object. You have no obligations to anyone else, so make sure this is written for your eyes only and not based on what someone else 'might think'. Notice the smile on your face as the pen moves and the **pictures move into your mind…**

_____
_____
_____
_____
_____
_____
_____
_____
_____
_____
_____
_____
_____
_____
_____
_____
_____
_____
_____

Worth A Thousand Words

Everything that you desire in life has a picture associated with it. We've already talked about how the mind likes pictures and it's time to take advantage of that fact once again. It's time to find those pictures and create a scrapbook or a collage so you have all of them in one place. This can involve, material things like cars and homes, dream holiday destinations; body's that you'd like to emulate, piles of cash, charity work, role models and more. You should be excited by whatever you see and you should be proud that you know that you can achieve everything that is pictured. **Do this as soon as possible.**

More Than Material Things

It goes without saying that most of us want nice things in this life, I have always loved cars and I see myself behind the wheel of a convertible Ferrari F430 in the future. However, I have realised as great as this is going to be; what is really exciting is *the person that I am going to have to become* (in accordance with my priorities) to obtain it. Once I have the keys in my hand I can be sure in the knowledge that I am a successful author, speaker and coach who has remained, loving, charitable and family orientated whilst improving his finances. Being this person is where the real excitement is not merely having the car. Think about it, we aren't human 'havings', we are human 'beings'.

Stop and Write it Down

Allow the pictures of all of the material things that you would buy if you won the lottery and realise that it is possible to get these things for yourself if you commit yourself to it. Write down everything that comes to mind and then next to it or below it, write down the type of person you'd have to become to get it.

The Return Of '4 Wheel Drive Goal Setting'

WARNING: you have read this before. If you don't want to create a fantastic future don't read it again. If you do, read on. Repetition deepens the impression

It is time to go back through the 4 Wheel Drive Goal Setting system in almost exactly the same way as you read it before. Why? It will be so strange for your mind to read the same thing in the same book twice that it will store it for sure. The only difference is we are going to set an ULTIMATE GOAL in one area of your life. This BIG goal will then be backed up by lots of little goals.

The 4 W's

The 4 "W's":

'What do I want, EXACTLY?'

'Why EXACTLY do I want it?'

'When EXACTLY do I want it by?'

'What MUST I do to get it?'

Let's start with **'What do I want, EXACTLY?'** – If you don't define what it is that you want, exactly; how is your mind supposed to get you there. If you wanted to drive to your hotel in Berlin from London, would you find the exact address of the hotel or would you just type 'Germany' into the satellite navigation system? Your mind works the same way; it needs to know EXACTLY where you want to go.

The MOST IMPORTANT wheel is: '**Why** EXACTLY do I want it?' You need to know WHY you want to achieve whatever it is that you want to achieve and it has to be powerful enough to get you to do things that you have to do EVEN when you don't feel like doing them. For example, let's say that you wanted to make an extra £200 per month: if the 'Why' was *"So I can pay off a bit more debt every month"* you are unlikely to create much momentum and ultimately not get there. What if the 'Why' was: *"So I can start my own business in an area that I have always been passionate about so I can eventually leave my job and do what I love every day"* – Do you see how this 'Why' is far more likely to create leverage and create lasting change?

Next is '**When EXACTLY do I want it by?**' You're brain needs an exact date to get you to take enough action at the right times. To use the holiday analogy again, imagine you said: "we're going on holiday next summer" and left it at that. How would you know when to pack? The answer is; you wouldn't! That is why the reality is you'd be saying something like: "we're going to New York on the 17th July 2014". Your mind would know that it has to do everything that it needs to do in preparation for the trip. Goals are the same.

The final element is: '**What MUST I do to get it?**' This wheel has the most freedom out of the wheels because you may not know everything that you have to do to achieve the goals but it will be vital for you to take an **abundance of action** and start as soon as possible! It is important that you work out what you are going to do first and find a plan, **a mentor** or a strategy, the most important thing is to GET MOVING! Be careful when planning what to do to get it because if you know EVERYTHING that you have to do to achieve the goal, you won't take enough action because you won't be inspired.

Putting it all together

Once you have gone through the above process of creating a goal you are left with something that should be phrased like the example below. Note, that the goal is stated in the PRESENT TENSE and in such a way that evokes positive feelings of it already being achieved; this magnetizes the subconscious mind to everything you'll need to do to achieve the goal. Once you have all of your goals written out this way it is important to review them at least once a day and I will go into detail on how to do this in the following pages.

Here is a goal that I recently achieved that should show you how it should be phrased:

"It is February 28th 2014 and I am so happy grateful that I easily completed my book The Lift your Life and it is published. This is an amazing achievement for me and it serves as a signpost in my life that I am really making happy progress every day within my dream career."

Which Goal Means the Most?

Stop and Write it Down

Now that the 4 wheel drive system is deeply embedded in your mind, it's time for you to pick an ultimate goal in a certain area of your life *and I mean huge*. Do not limit yourself at this point. Use the following areas of your life as ideas: **Health and fitness** (do you want to lose 40 pounds of fat and appear on the cover of *Men's* or *Women's Health* looking healthy and chiselled). **Relationships** (do you want to marry the man or woman of your dreams – what are they like?) **Finances** (Do you want a million, or ten million in the bank?) **Charity** (Do you want to create a multi million pound charity?) **Leisure** (Do you want to be a scratch golfer, or better?)

These are just ideas to make you think about the type of goal we are talking about here. This is a powerful process and I would say that this is one of the processes that I went through in the beginning that got me to where I am today.

'What do I want, EXACTLY?'

_____
_____
_____
_____
_____
_____
_____
_____
_____
_____
_____
_____
_____
_____
_____
_____
_____

'What do I want, EXACTLY?'

_____
_____
_____
_____
_____
_____
_____
_____
_____
_____
_____
_____
_____
_____
_____
_____

"What do I want, EXACTLY?'

_____
_____
_____
_____
_____
_____

"What do I want, EXACTLY?'

Now put the whole thing together as a sentence.

_____
_____
_____
_____
_____
_____
_____
_____
_____
_____
_____
_____
_____

Notice how great it feels to have your head filled with **pictures** of possibilities and dreams that are actually, already a step closer to reality. You will be setting the wheels in motion towards your fantastic future in the final chapter…

The Month that Changed your Life - Master Life in 30 Days

> *"Personal mastery is the discipline of continually clarifying and deepening our personal vision, of focusing our energies, of developing patience, and of seeing reality objectively."* PETER SENGE

This final chapter is what the whole book has been leading up to. It is less of a chapter and more of a short guide of how to approach the next 30 days so that all of the **knowledge** that you have gained is **acted upon** and you make progress towards the life of your dreams. The reading and writing you have done so far has already got you out of any 'mental rut' you may have been in. Your eyes have been opened to ideas and strategies that you didn't even know existed. It is now time to get used to implementing those strategies.

That little voice in your head is going to have a few things to say over the next 30 days. Be prepared! Realise that IT IS NOT YOU and make a decision to continue based on the life you desperately want.

The only thing that you need to do before you start is set your goals in every area of your life using the 4 wheel drive method. It also helps to give these areas of your life exciting names. For example: Health for me is *'Physical Power/World Class Health, Fitness and Muscularity'* and Finances is *'Absolute Financial Freedom'*. Set goals in the following areas (you can add more if you want to) Health, Career, Relationships, Finances, Spiritual, Charity/Contribution.

Once you have set at least one goal in every area of your life you can begin the 30 Day process to get you on a fast track to the life that you desire. When I first started telling people about this final chapter in the book they would say things like "you won't be able to get people to stick to anything as complicated as that for 30 days". I hadn't even told them what the process was!

Remember when I said that the chapters in this book would pretty much get progressively shorter. This one is no different.

All it is an outline of the fact that you will be doing the same thing EVERY DAY FOR 30 DAYS so I only need to write it out once.

I read a lot about daily routines during my own personal transformation and I have spent a lot of time deciding on what I believe gets the best results whilst being the easiest to do. It is a straight forward list of things to do based on the techniques that you have learned so far. It's so simple, fulfilling and motivating that the only thing that you will have to do is silence the voice in your head that tells you it's not for you. IT IS FOR YOU. It's for everyone. You'll understand why when you read it.

30 Days to The Rest of Your Life

> *"Make the rest of your life, the best of your life"*
> **ERIC THOMAS**

Tick every box on the below list every day for 30 days (you can go to jermaine-harris.com/30-days to download a copy of your 'future truths' and the checklist to print out every day.

Morning
- Get up 40 Minutes Earlier than usual
- Breathe Deeply
- Large Glass of Water (with add hydration enhancer if desired)
- 'Future Truths' said out loud with passion
- Visualize achieving Goals (Feel all the Feelings)

Rest of the Day
- Call/Text/Email at least two loved ones
- Read something that will improve you, your life or your career
- Spend 20 Minutes learning about a new passive income strategy

Evening
- Write a List of 10 Things you are truly grateful for
- Answer the question "What was Fantastic about today?"
- Answer the question "Who did I help today?"
- Answer the question "What did I learn today?"
- Plan Tomorrow
- 'Future Truths' said out loud with passion

The most important day of this whole process is DAY 31! You have well and truly lifted your life now. Are you going to continue living in this way and push on to create the ultimate vision of the healthy, happy prosperous lifestyle you deserve. Of course you are…

Conclusion

I want to congratulate you on taking the first step on the journey of self-improvement. You now have the ability to **decide** to stay on this path and create the life that you want. It was never my intention to write a 1000 page book with every personal development idea ever written in it. I wanted to introduce you to the simplest ideas that can help you to rapidly improve your life and I am proud to say that I think I have done that.

Now that you are on this journey, what I did want to do was point you in the direction of what I believe to be the best books, courses and products that will allow you to continue on this journey of improving your life and this is what you will find on the following pages.

Keep going and Keep growing.

Jermaine Harris

Grow on Instagram: @jermainecoach
Develop yourself on Youtube: youtube.com/jermaineharriscoach

It would be wonderful if you could pick your favourite part of this book and leave a positive review on Amazon.com if you have the time. It will allow me to help more and more people. Thank you so much.

Printed in Great Britain
by Amazon